Turkish

COOKING

Turkish

COOKING

AUTHENTIC CULINARY TRADITIONS FROM TURKEY

BADE JACKSON

CHARTWELL
BOOKS, INC.

A QUINTET BOOK

Published by Chartwell Books
A Division of Book Sales, Inc.
114, Northfield Avenue
Edison, New Jersey 08837

This edition produced for sale in the U.S.A., its
territories and dependencies only.

ISBN 0-7858-0918-X

This book was designed and produced by
Quintet Publishing Limited
6 Blundell Street
London N7 9BH

Creative Director: Richard Dewing
Art Director: Clare Reynolds
Designer: Steve West
Project Editor: Diana Steedman
Editor: Rosie Hankin
Food Stylist: Jennie Berresford
Photographer: Andrew Sydenham

Typeset in Great Britain by
Central Southern Typesetters, Eastbourne
Manufactured in Singapore by
Universal Graphics Pte Ltd
Printed in Singapore by
Star Standard Industries Pte Ltd

PICTURE CREDITS

The Publisher would like to thank the following for providing
photographs and for permission to reproduce copyright material:

Travel Ink/Abbie Enock: pages 6, 9, 10, 14, 15, 43, 89, 97;
Travel Ink/Luc Janssens: pages 8, 11, 12;
Papilio Photographic: pages 7, 13, 77;
Turkish Information Office, 170-173 Piccadilly, London: pages 27, 67.

Contents

Introduction

Good eating has always played an important role in the long history of the Turks. In Ottoman times they gave as much importance to the building of their kitchens as they did to the building of the palaces they catered for.

Early historical documents show that the basic structure of Turkish cuisine was already established during the nomadic period of the sixth to eleventh century AD, and in the first settled Turkish states of Asia, which were peopled by descendants of the tribes who fought with the Mongols in the thirteenth century. Culinary attitudes toward meat, dairy products, vegetables, and grains that characterized this period still make up the core of Turkish cuisine. The importance of the culinary art for the Ottoman sultans is evident to every visitor to Topkapi Palace. The huge kitchens were housed in several buildings under ten domes. By the seventeenth century, some thirteen hundred kitchen staff were housed in the palace.

Hundreds of cooks, specializing in different categories of dishes, such as soups, pilafs, kabobs, helva, beverages, and so on, fed as many as ten thousand people a day and, in addition, sent trays of food to others in the city as a royal favor. It was in this environment that hundreds of the Sultan's chefs, who dedicated their lives to their profession, developed and perfected the dishes of Turkish cuisine, which was then adopted by the kitchens of the provinces ranging from the Balkans to southern Russia, and down to North Africa. The spice route, the most important factor in culinary history, was under the full control of the Sultan and only the best ingredients were allowed to be traded under the strict standards established by the courts.

A cuisine of delicacy and richness

Turkey, with its long history of ancient civilizations, its fertile lands, and geographical setting between Asia and Europe, stretches a thousand miles from east to west, and covers an area equal to half the size of Mexico. It follows therefore that the cuisine of this country is diverse. The choice of dishes is wide, but all have a wonderful delicacy and richness.

Istanbul is well known for the richness and diversity of its cuisine as well as for its lavish entertainments. A fantastic variety of fresh fish from the Marmara Sea

Left: **For centuries the Topkapi Palace provided a rich backdrop to the feasting of the Ottoman sultans. Underneath the sumptuous courtyards lay the legendary kitchens, built in 1453, where thousands of chefs aimed for culinary perfection.**

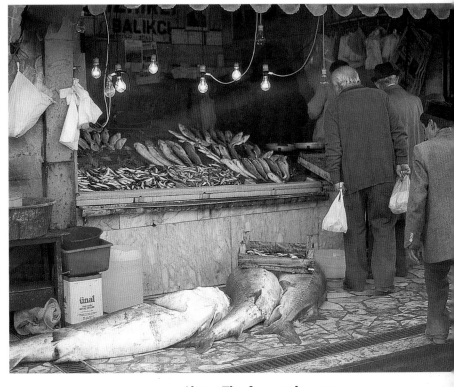

Above: **The famous bazaars are riots of color where huge quantities of produce change hands at furious pace. Here, locals hunt for bargains at the Calatasary Fish Market.**

and Black Sea, local high-quality vineyards, and an abundance of fresh produce as varied as olives, figs, fruit, and vegetables, combining with citizens from every corner of Turkey and beyond, make the list of recipes seem endless.

Turkey's Black Sea region, where the Anatolian plateau falls through vast forests of pine, fruit, and nut trees to a sea famous for its lobsters, caviar, and anchovies, is justly proud of its reputation for pasta and seafood dishes. Pasta or *makarna* is produced locally in a wide variety of forms, and contributes to many delicious specialties.

Eastern Turkey, bordering Georgia, Syria, Iran, and Iraq, with its high mountains, plains, and its ethnic mix, serves a variety of hot and spicy dishes. Using locally grown pistachios and exotic fruits, the eastern region is also famous for its desserts, such as widely known baklava and the local sherbets.

There are several types of sherbets made in Turkey. The traditonal varieties are still drinks that are made for special occasions such as the birth of a baby. They are made of sherbet candy which consists of traditonally dried and pressed fruits and flowers.

The southern region, with its lacelike coastline, contributes with mouthwatering Mediterranean dishes. Here there is an abundance of seafood, and a dazzling choice of local produce including fruits, nuts, olives, and vines.

Even at the center of Turkey, in the capital city of Ankara, surrounded by mountains, you can still buy an impressive variety of fresh fish, vegetables, and fruit daily. This is very important to the cook, as the use of frozen food is minimal, and the range of menus extensive. As each region has its specialties, so does each town, and each individual has his or her favorite dishes, but it is fair to say that the traditional Turkish household uses many of the recipes included in this book.

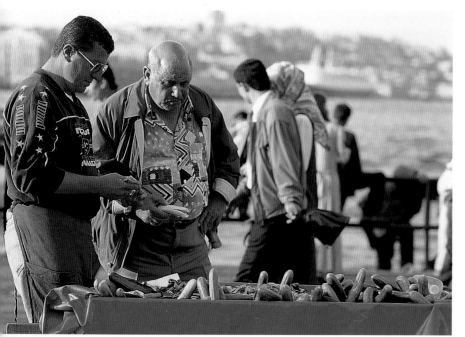

Above: Fresh vegetables, such as these cucumbers, are bought on a daily basis from traders for use in salads, *kabobs* and *dolmas*.

Turkish serving traditions

Turkish cooking takes time, effort, and organization. In Turkey food is bought fresh daily, and each meal of the day would be taken into account, with as much attention paid to breakfast as to lunch, supper, or dinner. As well as having a balance of nutrients, food should also be appealing to the eye, and, of course, tasty. Turkey, with its vast forests, fertile seas, and abundant lands, produces all the food to meet the country's needs. Her people are self-sufficient in all produce appreciate the natural goodness of organic food. Turkish cuisine is healthy and nutritious and the Turks are purist in their culinary taste; their dishes bring out the flavour of the main ingredient rather than hiding it behind sauces or spices, therefore spices and herbs are used very sparingly and singly.

Turkish people by nature like to be at the dinner table as long as possible, to enjoy their food to the maximum, to relax while eating it, and to converse over it. Appetisers form an important part of the cuisine. The kitchens of Topkapi Palace in Istanbul, dating from the Conqueror Fatih (1453), were decorated and fitted out in a manner worthy of their imperial function. The huge cauldron, the two great casseroles, together capable of containing several tons of food, and the gigantic soup ladles, which are all on display in their original places, are sufficient to point to the importance of soups in Turkish cuisine. It was in the same place that the janissaries, the élite soldiers of the Sultan's armies, received their thrice-yearly pay and swallowed down their legendary soup, as well as distributing palace *baklava* on feast days to the less fortunate.

Below: **Galata Bridge, spanning Istanbul's Golden Horn, is always filled with a dazzling array of hawkers, selling anything from sweet sherbet to roasted corn-on-the-cob.**

Appetizers

The tradition of serving four hot and four cold appetizers, preferably including a soup, is still very much alive in Turkey today. In the capital city of Ankara, all the restaurants still offer you a trolley full of cold and hot appetizers to choose from, before your main course is even ordered. During Ramadan, when Muslims fast throughout the day, only to eat in the evening at *iftar,* with all the Muslims in the world, the *iftar* tables would carry a menu of appetizers. Cheese, spinach, and meat boreks, soups, salads, rose petal and fig jams, cold dolmas, and, of course, olives to start, symbolize peace.

Turkish people are fond of cold appetizers that contain olive oil. We call them *zeytinyagli yemekler*: "olive oil dishes." The traditional Turkish family would think little of your cooking if you did not serve at least two hot and two cold appetizers, with a salad.

Cooking with olive oil is also a good way of preserving vegetables. They will keep, covered, in the fridge for a few days, although it is recommended that any recipes with a flavoring such as garlic added to the olive oil should not be kept more than 12 hours, as there can be a danger of botulism after this time. It is also recommended that a high-quality olive oil is used, a good indication of this being the price paid for the oil.

You do not have to go as far as the pastry houses or restaurants to be offered a choice of appetizers in modern Turkey. Even traveling by train, you can still expect to be served with delicious *sigara borek,* cold dolmas, and salads, before ordering your main course.

Above: **Turkish rugs hang from the walls of the covered market (Kapali Carsi).**

Kabobs and Dolmas

Kebap is another category of food which is typically Turkish, dating back to the times when the nomadic Turks learned to grill and roast their meat over the campfires. Given the numerous types of kebaps, it helps to realize that you categorize them by the way the meat is cooked, as in *sis kebap* and *doner kebap.* It is not that they are complicated or even particularly exotic, but their basic flavor and combination of simple ingredients has stood the test of time. The preparation of doner kebap always follows the traditional methods. First the boned leg of lamb is marinated with herbs, yogurt, tomato, and onions for a few hours, then it is sliced thinly, and wrapped around a vertical spit and placed in front of a three-tiered broiler. As the spit revolves slowly, the outside layer of the lamb cooks. From this revolving action the dish takes its name *doner,* which means "to turn" in Turkish. Sis kebap is another way of cooking meat. *Sis* means

skewer in Turkish. In Nomadic times the meat was cooked slowly over the camp fires along with onions, peppers and herbs. It should be noted that the unique taste of kebaps is due more to the breeds of sheep and cattle which are raised in open pastures, than to their special marinades and the way of cooking.

Dolma is the generic term for stuffed vegetables, being a derivative of the verb *doldurmak*, meaning "to fill," it actually means "stuffed" in Turkish. There are two types of dolma: those filled with a ground meat mix and those filled with a rice mix. The latter are cooked in olive oil and eaten at room temperature. The meat dolma is a main course dish, eaten with a yogurt sauce, and is frequently prepared in an average household.

Left: **Colorful cherry-juice sellers clad in tarbooshes offer round-the-clock refreshment for thirsty diners.**

Desserts and Drinks

The most common dessert served is seasonal fruits that acquire their unique taste from the abundance of sun and the traditional methods of cultivation. For most of the spring and summer, fruit is eaten fresh. Later on into the fall, the fruit may be used dried, in compotes, or made into preserves. Among the special preserves are marmalades, made from quince or sour cherries, and those prepared using figs or delicate rose petals.

There is not a spot with a view, or a park in Turkey without its tea or coffee house. A great deal has been written about Turkish coffee, its history, its significance in social life and the ambience of the coffee houses, and yet the tiny brew with its annoying grounds can be a disappointment to the uninitiated. A few words of caution—the grounds are not to be swallowed! Secondly, do not expect a caffeine surge—it is not strong coffee, just thick. And, remember, it is actually the setting and the company that matter: the coffee is just an excuse for an occasion to socialize.

Other beverages that are distinctly Turkish are *Boza,* a thick, fermented drink made from wheat berries; *Sahlep,* a hot drink made with powdered roots of certain orchids; *Ayran,* a refreshing drink made with yogurt and the many excellent bottled pure fruit juices.

Above: **The panels of the Sultan's Harem in Topkapi Palace are stunning displays of Turkish handcraftman's skills.**

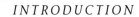
Afiyet Olsun

In the following recipes, I have tried to include a wide variety of meat and vegetable dishes—many that would be prepared in an average Turkish household, and other more unusual recipes—all with easily available ingredients. All the dishes in this book are tried and tested. In most cases you will have no difficulty obtaining all the ingredients, and where there is any doubt you will find alternative suggestions. I hope you will enjoy the dishes as much as we do, and, as we say in Turkey, *Afiyet Olsun*, which means "good appetite."

Jade J. Jackson

Soups
and
Salads

CORBALAR
VE SALATALAR

Yogurt Soup

YOGURT CORBASI

This is the kind of soup that you can serve to someone who is feeling a little "under the weather." It is still called in some regions hasta corbasi *which means "soup for the ill." The ingredients differ slightly from region to region, but I prefer this version which is a cross between yogurt and yayla soup. Yayla soup can be literally translated as "soup from the valley" and is exactly the same as Yogurt Soup with the addition, while simmering, of a grated tomato.*

Tip

Turkish yogurts are thick and creamy and very similar to Greek yogurt. In all the recipes calling for yogurt, use a plain, thick, unsweetened set yogurt.

Serves 4

1 Tbsp butter or margarine

1 Tbsp flour

Generous 1 cup plain yogurt, strained

4 cups chicken stock

1 Tbsp rice, washed and drained (optional)

Salt and ground black pepper

Dried mint and paprika, to garnish

Croûtons, to serve

PREPARATION TIME: **5 MINUTES**
COOKING TIME: **25 MINUTES**

1 Heat the butter or margarine in a large saucepan and add the flour. Stirring continuously, brown gently over medium heat until smooth.

2 Mix in the yogurt, and stir throughly, then slowly add the chicken stock.

3 Bring to a boil and add the rice, if using. Season well, cover, and simmer gently for about 15 minutes, or until the rice is soft. Garnish with dried mint and paprika, and serve hot with croûtons.

Ezo Bride Soup

EZO GELIN CORBASI

This soup has its origins in an ancient folkloric tale. According to the story the soup was cooked in celebration of the wedding of Ezo, a chieftan's beautiful daughter, who was married near a famous bridge over the river Kizil Irmak. The story has an unhappy ending, so I will not disclose it to avoid putting you off this fine soup.

Serves 4

½ stick butter plus a little extra

1 small onion, chopped

5 cups chicken stock

⅔ cup bulgur wheat

½ cup red lentils

1 Tbsp tomato paste

Salt and ground black pepper

2 tsp paprika

PREPARATION TIME: **10 MINUTES**
COOKING TIME: **30 MINUTES**

1 Heat the ½ stick butter in a saucepan and fry the onion. Pour in the chicken stock and bring to a boil.

2 Add the bulgur wheat, red lentils, and tomato paste. Stir, then simmer for 20 minutes over low heat. Taste and adjust the seasoning if necessary.

3 Just before serving, melt a teaspoon of butter in a skillet, stir in the paprika, and then pour over the soup.

Wedding Soup

DUGUN CORBASI

This is a delicious soup that is traditionally served at weddings. However, it is not necessary to wait for a wedding among your family or friends to enjoy it!

Tip

If you cannot find mutton, substitute lamb. The dish will not be so full flavored but it will still be delicious.

Serves 4

9 oz mutton, diced fine

1 onion, peeled and left whole

1 carrot, peeled and left whole

5 cups water

¼ stick butter

1 Tbsp flour

2 small eggs

Juice of 1 lemon

1 tsp paprika or chili powder

Salt and ground black pepper

PREPARATION TIME: **10 MINUTES**
COOKING TIME: **35 MINUTES**

1 Place the meat, onion, and carrot in a saucepan with the water, cover, and bring to a boil. Simmer gently for 1 hour. Discard the onion and carrot.

2 Melt half the butter in another pan, add the flour, and brown lightly. Slowly pour in the prepared stock and bring to a boil. Cover and simmer for 20 minutes until the meat is tender.

3 Break the eggs into a bowl, add the lemon juice, and beat well. Carry on beating the mixture while adding, little by little, a tablespoon of the soup. Pour the mixture into the soup, stirring continuously. Turn off the heat.

4 Melt the remaining butter in a small skillet, stir in the paprika or chili powder, then pour over the soup. Season well and serve.

Behind every good soup, stew or sauce is a well-made stock. Stock cubes, while convenient, are usually over salty. Homemade stocks are simple to make and enhance your recipes beyond measure. As for fish and vegetable—you can vary the ingredients according to your taste. It is just a matter of placing the ingredients in a saucepan of cold water and simmering gently for 1 to 2 hours. Store your supply in the freezer in varying quantities, ready to hand.

Chicken Stock

PREPARATION TIME: **5 MINUTES**
COOKING TIME: **1 HOUR MINIMUM**

a chicken carcass
2 leeks, white parts only, washed
1 large onion, peeled and quartered
2 carrots, washed
several sprigs of parsley
3 celery stalks
6 black peppercorns
6 pints water

1 Place all the ingredients in a large pan. Pour in the water, cover, and slowly bring to a boil. Skim off the fat and foam.
2 Simmer, covered, for at least 1 hour. Strain, cool and store either in the refrigerator or in the freezer.

Meat Stock

PREPARATION TIME: **10 MINUTES**
COOKING TIME: **2 HOURS MINIMUM**

1 lb beef pieces, coarsely chopped
2 leeks, white parts only, washed
1 large onion, peeled and halved
2 carrots, washed
several sprigs of parsley
1 garlic clove
6 pints water
6 black peppercorns

1 Place all the vegetables and meat in a large pan, pour in the water and slowly bring to a boil. Skim off the fat and foam. Add the black peppercorns, and simmer, covered, for at least 2 hours, topping up with a little water as necessary and skimming occasionally.
2 Strain, cool and store either in the refrigerator or in the freezer.

Chicken and Noodle Soup

SEHRIYE CORBASI

This soup is very popular with children and is a good way of introducing them to soup. The crafty addition of star-shaped noodles, or something similar, will entice them to try at least just a spoonful.

Serves 4

¼ stick butter

5 oz chicken, chopped fine

2 fresh ripe tomatoes, chopped

3½ cups chicken stock

1 carrot, diced

2 oz noodles

Salt and ground black pepper

Juice of ½ lemon

Chopped fresh parsley,
   to garnish

PREPARATION TIME: **5 MINUTES**
COOKING TIME: **25 MINUTES**

1 Melt the butter in a saucepan and fry the chicken for 1 minute.

2 Add the tomatoes, stir, and pour in the chicken stock. Bring to a boil, then add the carrot and noodles. Cover and simmer for 20 minutes.

3 Just before serving, season well and add the lemon juice. Serve hot, garnished with chopped parsley.

Lentil Soup

MERCIMEK CORBASI

This is one of my favorite winter soups, and it is both nourishing and satisfying. The addition of cumin is an Anatolian variation that gives a distinctive taste.

Serves 4

1 Tbsp butter or margarine

1 small onion, chopped

1 carrot, diced

3½ cups chicken stock

Scant 1 cup green lentils

1 tsp ground cumin

Salt and ground black pepper

Chopped fresh parsley,
    to garnish (optional)

PREPARATION TIME: **5 MINUTES**
COOKING TIME: **25 MINUTES**

1 Heat the butter and fry the onion until soft. Add the carrot and cook for 1 minute.

2 Pour in the chicken stock and add the lentils. Bring to a boil over medium heat and stir in the cumin. Simmer for 20 minutes. Pass soup through a metal sifter, or purée in a blender or food processor.

3 Return to the pan, reheat, taste and adjust the seasoning, and serve with parsley scattered over, if using.

Green Salad

YESIL SALATA

This is a very basic salad, but nevertheless often used in Turkish cooking especially with grilled meats. The basis of the salad is green lettuce, hence the given name, but it is usually made as follows.

Serves 4

8 oz mixed salad leaves

2 scallions, chopped

2 fresh tomatoes, sliced

3 radishes, sliced

2 hard-cooked eggs

2 Tbsp each chopped fresh dill weed and parsley

3 or 4 black olives, pitted and chopped

1½ Tbsp olive oil

1½ Tbsp lemon juice

Salt and ground black pepper

Feta cheese cubes, to garnish

PREPARATION TIME: **15 MINUTES**

1 Wash the salad leaves, dry in a salad spinner or clean dish towel, and put into a large salad bowl. Arrange the scallions, sliced tomatoes, and radishes over the salad leaves.

2 Cut the eggs into wedges lengthwise. Add to the salad bowl, along with the dill weed, parsley, and olives.

3 To make the dressing, combine the olive oil, lemon juice, and seasoning to taste. Then pour over the salad. Garnish with small cubes of feta cheese before serving.

Bean Salad

PIYAZ

In most Turkish streets you can find a kofte *restaurant where this salad would be most popular. Use any type of white bean you like in this dish, although fava beans will disintegrate a bit. Check the package for cooking times.*

Serves 4

Generous 1 cup navy beans

2 tomatoes, chopped

1 green bell pepper or chile, chopped

1 onion, chopped

A handful of fresh parsley, chopped

Salt and ground black pepper

2 hard-cooked eggs

3 radishes, sliced

1 Tbsp red wine vinegar

1 Tbsp olive oil

4 black olives, to garnish

PREPARATION TIME: **OVERNIGHT PLUS 20 MINUTES**

1 Soak the beans overnight, drain, and place in a saucepan with plenty of water. Bring to a boil and simmer until tender. Drain, rinse in cold water, and drain again. Place in a serving dish and add the tomatoes and bell pepper or chile.

2 In a separate bowl rub the onion with a little salt, then wash, and drain. Add the onion to the salad, along with the parsley, and season to taste.

3 Cut the eggs lengthwise into wedges. Arrange the eggs and the radishes over the salad.

4 Mix the vinegar with the olive oil, and pour over the salad. Garnish with olives and serve.

Eggplant Salad with Yogurt

YOGURTLU PATLICAN SALATA

This salad is very well known in Turkey as it is usually served with the potent Turkish spirit, Raki. It is served everywhere from a seaside bar to a five-star hotel.

Serves 4

2 eggplants
¾ cup plain yogurt
2 garlic cloves, crushed
1 green bell pepper, seeded, grilled until soft, and chopped
1 large fresh tomato, peeled and chopped
1 Tbsp olive oil
Juice of 1 lemon
Salt and ground black pepper
A few black olives

PREPARATION TIME: **40 MINUTES**

1 Prepare the eggplants in the same way as for Eggplant Salad (see page 24). Once peeled, mash the flesh, and place in a salad bowl.

2 Stir in the yogurt, garlic, bell pepper, and tomato.

3 Combine the olive oil and lemon juice to make the dressing, adding seasoning to taste. Pour over the salad and garnish with a few olives.

Houmous

HUMUS

This is the traditional Turkish version of the well-known salad, and is quite a different taste than a shop-bought one. If you cannot find tahini (ground sesame seeds) in your supermarket, try a specialty shop or a delicatessen.

Serves 4

Generous 1 cup garbanzo beans
½ cup tahini
1 garlic clove, crushed
2 Tbsp lemon juice
1 Tbsp olive oil
½ tsp paprika
Salt and ground black pepper
Crackers or toasted bread, to serve

PREPARATION TIME: **OVERNIGHT PLUS 2 HOURS**

1 Soak the garbanzo beans overnight, drain well, and put in a saucepan with plenty of water to cover. Bring to a boil and simmer until soft, about 2½ hours. (Skinned garbanzo beans will cook in about 1½ hours.)

2 Remove the skins from the garbanzo beans and mash until smooth, adding a little water if necessary.

3 Add the rest of the ingredients, and season to taste. Mix well and place in a serving dish. Serve with crackers or toasted bread.

Bulgur Wheat Salad

KISIR

This is a very nutritious and filling salad. It is probably a good idea , therefore, to serve it with a light meal, such as simply grilled meat.

Serves 4

1½ cups bulgur wheat
1 Tbsp tomato paste
4 scallions, trimmed and chopped
A handful of fresh mint, chopped
A handful of fresh parsley, chopped
Juice of 1 lemon
Salt and ground black pepper
2 Romaine lettuce leaves, torn

PREPARATION TIME: **20 MINUTES**

1 Place the bulgur wheat in a bowl and cover with boiling water. Soak for 5 minutes, or until the water is absorbed.

2 Stir in the tomato paste. When thoroughly mixed, add the scallions and herbs.

3 Pour over the lemon juice, taste, and season with salt and pepper. Serve garnished with the torn lettuce leaves.

Eggplant Salad

PATLICAN SALATA

This is one of my favorite salads. It is traditionally cooked over an open fire to accompany grilled meats. You can prepare it using the range if you don't mind the mess.

Serves 4

1 eggplant
1 large fresh tomato, peeled and chopped
1 green bell pepper, sliced fine
1 large garlic clove, crushed
1 onion, chopped
Salt and ground black pepper
A handful of fresh parsley, chopped
Juice of 1 lemon
1 Tbsp olive oil

PREPARATION TIME: **40 MINUTES**

Tip

When raw onion appears in a recipe, chop or slice it as required, then rub a little salt into it. Then wash and drain before adding to the dish. This softens the onion slightly, making it much more palatable.

1 Wash the eggplant and prick all over with a fork. Place on the grill (before the meat as it takes longer to cook). To make sure it cooks evenly, turn it occasionally using the stem as a handle. When the skin of the eggplant looks quite burnt, make sure the flesh is soft right through by testing it with a fork.

2 Hold the eggplant under cold running water to cool, then peel the skin, leaving the soft flesh. Slice it into a serving dish and add the tomatoes, bell pepper, and garlic.

3 Place the onion in a separate dish and rub with a good pinch of salt, then wash and drain. Add to the salad along with the parsley.

4 To make the dressing, combine the lemon juice, olive oil, and salt and pepper to taste. Drizzle over the salad and serve.

Yogurt Hors d'Oeuvres

CACIK

This dish is often served with four or five other appetizers at the beginning of any meal, and while it is used as a dip in some countries, in Turkey it is served in individual bowls and eaten with a spoon.

Serves 4

Scant 2 cups plain yogurt
2 garlic cloves, crushed
1 small or a ½ large cucumber
1 Tbsp dried mint
1 Tbsp dried dill weed
1 tsp olive oil
A few fresh mint leaves and ice cubes, to garnish

PREPARATION TIME: **10 MINUTES**

1 Place the yogurt in a bowl and add the garlic.

2 Peel the cucumber and dice fine. Stir into the yogurt with the dried herbs. Mix well and add a little water if the *cacik* is too thick.

3 Sprinkle with the olive oil and serve, garnished with mint leaves and ice cubes.

Shepherd's Salad

COBAN SALATA

This salad owes its origins to the meal that a shepherd would take for his mid-day meal. The simple ingredients of onion, tomato, cucumber and bell pepper would be garnished with herbs that he might gather from the mountainside. My recipe is a formalized version enjoyed in the city.

Serves 4

1 onion

Salt and ground black pepper

2 large fresh tomatoes

1 small cucumber

1 green bell pepper, seeded and
   diced

1 chile, diced fine (optional)

A handful of fresh parsley,
   chopped

A handful of fresh dill weed
   (optional)

1 Tbsp olive oil

1 Tbsp lemon juice

A few black olives, to garnish

PREPARATION TIME: **15 MINUTES**

1 Slice the onion into thin half circles. Place in a bowl and rub with a little salt, then wash, and drain.

2 Chop the tomatoes and place in a serving dish with the onions.

3 Peel the cucumber, dice, and add to the bowl.

4 Stir in the bell pepper, chile, if using, and the herbs.

5 Drizzle the salad with the olive oil and lemon juice, season to taste, and serve garnished with olives.

French Beans Cooked in Olive Oil
ZEYTINYAGLI FASULYE

Beans Cooked in Olive Oil
BAKLA

Leeks Cooked in Olive Oil
ZEYTINYAGLI PIRASA

Fava Bean Mold
FAVA

Eggplant Cooked in Olive Oil
PATLICAN IMAM BAYILDI

Circassian Chicken
CERKEZ TAVUGU

Potatoes with Cheese
PEYNIRLI PATATES

Albanian Liver
ARNAVUT CIGERI

Cigarette Pies
SIGARA BOREGI

Fried Vegetables
KIZARTMA

Cold Stuffed Bell Peppers
ZEYTINYAGLI BIBER DOLMASI

Stuffed Grape Leaves
ZEYTINYAGLI YAPRAK DOLMASI

Stuffed Cabbage Leaves
ZEYTINYAGLI LAHANA DOLMASI

Mussel Casserole
MIDYE PILAKI

Stuffed Mussels
MIDYE DOLMA

Fried Mussels
MIDYE TAVA

Cold and Hot Appetizers

BASLANGICLAR
SOGUK MEZELER
VE SICAK MEZELER

French Beans Cooked in Olive Oil

ZEYTINYAGLI FASULYE

This is a very common olive oil appetizer to be served with almost any meat dish.

Serves 4

Generous ½ cup olive oil

1 onion, chopped

1 lb French beans, trimmed

1 large fresh tomato, skinned
  and chopped

1 Tbsp tomato paste

Salt and ground black pepper

Chopped fresh parsley,
  to garnish

PREPARATION TIME: **15 MINUTES**
COOKING TIME: **30 MINUTES**

1 Heat the oil in a skillet and fry the onions until transparent, then add the beans, and fry together for a few minutes.

2 Cover with cold water, then add the chopped tomato. Bring to a boil and stir in the tomato paste, then reduce the heat, and simmer for 20 minutes, or until the beans are cooked. Drain, retaining about 1 tablespoon of the cooking juice.

3 Transfer the beans to a glass dish and add the retained juice. Season to taste. Chill before serving, garnished with parsley.

Beans Cooked in Olive Oil

BAKLA

This is a very nutritious dish, and the brightness of the beans is much improved by the addition of the dill, especially if it is fresh.

Serves 4

½ cup olive oil

2 lb fresh fava beans

1 large onion, cut into rings

1 Tbsp chopped fresh dill weed

1 Tbsp sugar

Juice of 1 lemon

Salt and ground black pepper

1 Tbsp chopped fresh parsley

Plain yogurt, to serve

PREPARATION TIME: **20 MINUTES**
COOKING TIME: **1 HOUR 10 MINUTES**

1 Heat the oil in a saucepan, stir in the beans, and fry for a few minutes.

2 Line another saucepan with half the onion rings and place the beans evenly on top. Layer the remaining onions on top of the beans and add the dill weed, sugar, lemon juice, seasoning, and 1½ cups water. Cover with waxed paper and cook for about 1 hour, or until tender. If the beans are canned they will require less cooking time. Remove from heat and allow to cool.

3 Transfer to a serving dish and scatter parsley over. Serve with plain yogurt.

Leeks Cooked in Olive Oil

ZEYTINYAGLI PIRASA

Although this sounds a rather humble dish, it is quite popular and is surprisingly refreshing with the combination of freshly squeezed lemon juice, leeks and carrots cooked in extra virgin olive oil.

Serves 4

Generous ½ cup olive oil
1 onion, chopped
1 lb leeks, chopped
1 carrot, sliced
Generous ½ cup long grain rice, washed and drained
1 tomato, skinned and chopped
1 tsp sugar
Salt and ground black pepper
Juice of ½ lemon
Lemon wedges, to serve

PREPARATION TIME: **15 MINUTES**
COOKING TIME: **25 MINUTES**

1 Heat the oil in a saucepan and fry the onion until soft. Then add the leeks, carrots, and rice, and fry together for a few minutes, stirring occasionally.

2 Add water to cover and bring to a boil over medium heat. Add the tomato, sugar, and seasoning to taste, then reduce the heat, and simmer, covered, for 20 minutes, until the water is reduced by half and the rice is cooked.

3 Allow to cool, then place in a serving dish. Sprinkle with the lemon juice and serve with lemon wedges for squeezing over.

Fava Bean Mold

FAVA

Fava beans might be difficult to obtain from a supermarket. They are sometimes known as broad beans. You may be able to get them from a delicatessen or, if not, then any dried beans will do. The finished dish might not be as firm as it is supposed to be, but it will taste just as good.

Serves 4

Generous 2¾ cups dried fava beans

1¼ cups olive oil, plus extra to glaze

1 onion, quartered

1 tsp sugar

Juice of 1 lemon

Salt and ground black pepper

Chopped fresh parsley, to garnish

PREPARATION TIME:
OVERNIGHT PLUS 10 MINUTES
COOKING TIME:
45 MINUTES PLUS CHILLING TIME

1 Soak the beans overnight.

2 Heat the oil in a saucepan and fry the onion for a few minutes. Add 2½ cups water, or just enough water to cover the onions, and bring to a boil.

3 Drain the beans and add to the onions. Simmer for 10 minutes then add the sugar, lemon juice, and seasoning. Simmer the mixture for 30 minutes more, or until the beans are tender.

4 Purée the beans with a little of the cooking water by pressing them through a metal sieve with a wooden spoon, or use a blender or food processor, and place in an oiled 7-inch ring mold.

5 Chill for 2 hours. When chilled, place a serving plate over the mold, invert, and turn out the purée. Brush with a little olive oil and garnish with parsley.

Tip

Cooking dried beans and peas in a pressure cooker reduces the cooking time dramatically. Always refer to the instructions on the package.

Eggplant Cooked in Olive Oil

PATLICAN IMAM BAYILDI

Eggplant is a special favorite in Turkey. There are said to be over a hundred ways of cooking it! Many of these have picturesque names, like imam bayildi, *translated as the "Imam fainted," presumably from delight at such a delicious dish, or maybe the description of the striped eggplant resembles the Imam lying down in his traditional clothes.*

Serves 3

3 eggplants
1¼ cups olive oil
1 onion, chopped
2 large, fresh ripe tomatoes, skinned and chopped
1 garlic clove, crushed
Juice of ½ lemon
1 tsp sugar
Salt and ground black pepper
3 firm, fresh tomatoes, sliced
Chopped fresh parsley, to garnish

PREPARATION TIME: **20 MINUTES**
COOKING TIME: **45 MINUTES**

1 Peel the eggplant skin in stripes lengthwise. Cut a slit in the eggplants and scoop out most of the flesh, being careful not to pierce the skin. Discard the flesh.

2 Heat 1 tablespoon of the olive oil in a heatproof casserole and fry the eggplants for a few minutes, until nicely colored.

3 Pour the remaining oil into a saucepan, and fry the onions until soft. Stir in the chopped tomatoes and garlic, and fry together for a few minutes.

4 Drain the eggplants, fill with the vegetable mixture, then return to the casserole, slit side up, with enough water to cover. Stir in the lemon juice, sugar, and salt and pepper to taste. Cover and simmer for about 15 minutes over medium heat.

5 Place a sliced tomato on each eggplant and simmer for 10 minutes more over low heat, until the eggplants are soft but retain their shape. Allow to cool, then place in a serving dish, and garnish with parsley.

Circassian Chicken

CERKEZ TAVUGU

Circassia, situated on the Black Sea on the north of the Caucasus mountains, was a region famous in the times of the Ottoman Empire for its horses, horsemen and horsewomen. The game of "Cirit," similar to polo, was imported to Istanbul along with this famous recipe.

Serves 6

1 small fresh chicken
1 onion, sliced
Salt and ground black pepper
1 lb walnuts, shelled and peeled
6 cups fresh bread crumbs
1 tsp chili powder or paprika
Olive oil, to glaze
Chopped hot chile, to garnish

PREPARATION TIME: **20 MINUTES**
COOKING TIME: **60 MINUTES**

1 Wash the chicken and place it in a large saucepan with the onion. Pour enough water to cover and bring to a boil. Simmer for about 40 minutes, depending on the size of the chicken, until well cooked.

2 When cooked, reserve the stock, and skin and bone the chicken. Chop the meat into very small pieces and place in a serving dish. Season with salt and pepper.

3 Put the walnuts in a blender or food processor and chop fine. Then add half the bread crumbs and half the chili powder or paprika. Blend for 1 minute, then add the rest of the bread crumbs and spice, and blend thoroughly.

4 Place the mixture in a mixing bowl and stir in some of the reserved chicken stock until it reaches the consistency of heavy cream.

5 Place half the chicken pieces in the serving dish, cover with the sauce and sprinkle the remaining chicken pieces over the top. Brush with a little olive oil and sprinkle with chopped fresh chile.

Tip

To peel walnuts, soak them in boiling water and leave until the water cools down. The peel will come away easily, but it is important to carry out the task as soon as they are cool enough to handle, otherwise a bitter flavor is imparted to the nut.

Potatoes With Cheese

PEYNIRLI PATATES

This is a very light dish and can be served as a snack or as a side dish.

Serves 4

5⅓ cups mashed potato

1 cup shredded Cheddar cheese

1 stick butter

Salt and ground black pepper

3 eggs

PREPARATION TIME: **20 MINUTES**
COOKING TIME: **25 MINUTES**

1 Preheat a 400°F oven. Place the mashed potato with the cheese, butter, and seasoning in a large bowl and mix thoroughly, gradually folding in two of the eggs.

2 Shape the mixture into a cylinder and cut into circles. Place on a greased cookie sheet and brush with egg yolk. Cook for about 20 minutes, until golden. Serve hot.

Albanian Liver

ARNAVUT CIGERI

Make sure you use lamb's liver for this dish. Ox liver can be substituted but it requires long, slow cooking and is therefore not so suitable.

Serves 4

Olive oil, for shallow frying

2 Tbsp flour

Salt and ground black pepper

9 oz lamb's liver, diced

1 bunch scallions, chopped

2 Tbsp chopped fresh parsley

PREPARATION TIME: **15 MINUTES**
COOKING TIME: **25 MINUTES**

1 Heat the oil in a large skillet. Place the flour in a bowl and stir in some seasoning. Dip each piece of liver in the flour, shake off the excess, and fry in the pan. Turn occasionally for even coloring. Do not overcook as this would harden and dry the liver.

2 Drain, place in a warm serving dish, and garnish with scallions and parsley. Serve immediately.

Cigarette Pies

SIGARA BOREGI

This is one of my favorite appetizers and it can be rolled in advance. Simply sprinkle the pies with flour to prevent sticking, cover, and keep in the refrigerator for later use.

Serves 4

8 oz phyllo pastry, fresh
or frozen
Olive oil, for shallow frying

FOR THE FILLING
$2\frac{2}{3}$ cups mashed potato
1 onion, chopped fine
2 oz Cheddar cheese, shredded
2 Tbsp chopped fresh parsley
Pinch of paprika
Salt and ground black pepper

PREPARATION TIME: **30 MINUTES**
COOKING TIME: **30 MINUTES**

Tip

You can make this borek using different fillings, too. Try feta cheese with some chopped fresh parsley and seasoning or a filling of ground beef or lamb cooked with some chopped onion.

1 On a floured board, cut phyllo pastry into 3-inch triangles. Keep them under a damp dish towel to prevent them from becoming brittle.

2 Mix all the filling ingredients together in a bowl and season well. Place 1 teaspoon of the stuffing at the center of one side of the triangle, fold the two corners over

the stuffing, then roll like a cigarette, sealing the edge with a little water. Repeat with all the remaining pastry sheets.

3 Heat the oil in a skillet and fry the boreks on all sides until golden. Place in a serving dish lined with waxed paper, to absorb the excess oil, and serve while still hot.

Fried Vegetables

KIZARTMA

This is a very colorful dish and can be made in advance and kept in the refrigerator for a few hours. It is just as good cold or hot. You can use a variety of vegetables for different tastes.

Serves 4

Olive oil, for shallow frying
1 eggplant, peeled and sliced into rings
1 large potato, peeled and sliced
2 green or red bell peppers, pricked
2 mild chiles, pricked
1 zucchini, sliced
Flour, for coating
3 fresh ripe tomatoes, chopped
1 Tbsp chopped parsley
1 garlic clove, crushed
Plain yogurt, to serve

PREPARATION TIME: **20 MINUTES**
COOKING TIME: **30 MINUTES**

1 Heat the oil in a skillet or wok and fry the eggplant, turning once to make sure both sides are the same color. Line a dish with paper towels to absorb the excess oil. Place the eggplant slices in the dish as they are cooked. Then fry the potatoes in the same way and add to the lined dish.

2 Fry the whole bell peppers and chiles, covering the pan with a lid to prevent hot oil spitting.

3 Dip the zucchini in a little flour, shake off the excess, and fry until nicely browned. Now transfer all the vegetables to a serving dish.

4 Heat a little oil in a separate skillet and add the chopped tomatoes and garlic. Fry for a few minutes. Pour this sauce over the vegetables and serve with plain yogurt. Garnish with chopped parsley.

Stuffing for Vegetables

DOLMA ICI

Here is the basic stuffing recipe for soguk colmalar *'cold stuffed vegetables.'*

Serves 5

PREPARATION TIME: **10 MINUTES**
COOKING TIME: **15 MINUTES**

1¼ cups olive oil
1 large onion, chopped
1 Tbsp pine nuts
Generous 1 cup long grain rice, washed and drained
1 Tbsp small raisins, soaked and washed
Salt and ground black pepper
1 tsp sugar
14 fl oz water
Juice of 1 lemon
A handful of fresh parsley, chopped
2 tsp chopped fresh dill weed
2 tsp chopped fresh mint
1 tsp ground cinnamon

1 Heat the oil in a large saucepan, stir in the onions and pine nuts, and fry for a few minutes, until the pine nuts are light pink in color.

2 Add the rice and stir together until the rice becomes transparent. Add the raisins, salt and pepper, sugar, and water to cover. Cover and cook until the water is absorbed.

3 Allow to cool slightly then stir in the lemon juice, parsley, dill weed, and mint.

Cold Stuffed Bell Peppers

ZEYTINYAGLI BIBER
DOLMASI

Use any color bell pepper you like for this dish. Red and yellow ones are sweeter than green. Or how about a variety for a really eye-catching presentation?

Serves 5

5 bell peppers
1 quantity stuffing (see above)
1 large fresh tomato, sliced horizontally into 5
Juice of ½ lemon

PREPARATION TIME: **20 MINUTES**
COOKING TIME: **25 MINUTES**

1 Wash the bell peppers, cut out the stalk and scoop out the seeds. Fill the bell peppers with the stuffing and cover each one with a slice of tomato.

2 Place standing up in a saucepan. The pan should be just big enough to accommodate them yet snug enough to retain their shapes while cooking. Pour a little water into the pan, to a level 2 inches below the pepper top, and place a small heatproof plate over the bell peppers. Cook over medium heat for 15 minutes, until the peppers are softened but still intact. Allow to cool in the saucepan then place in a serving dish and sprinkle with lemon juice.

Cold Stuffed Bell Peppers ▶

Stuffed Grape Leaves

ZEYTINYAGLI YAPRAK

DOLMASI

This is a very popular starter although it is quite time consuming. The grape leaves may be fresh or canned for this dish. You will need the juice of a second lemon and a pinch of salt to prepare fresh leaves.

Serves 4

9 oz grape leaves, fresh or
canned

1 quantity stuffing (see page 36)

Generous ½ cup olive oil

Juice of 1 lemon

1 tsp sugar

Lemon wedges, to serve

PREPARATION TIME: **1 HOUR**
COOKING TIME: **1 HOUR**

1 If using fresh leaves, wash them thoroughly, place in a saucepan, and cover with water. Add the juice of 1 lemon and a pinch of salt. Bring to a boil, cover the pan, and simmer for 20 minutes. If using canned leaves, wash them and put them in a saucepan with plenty of water. Bring to a boil and simmer for 5 minutes. Allow to cool slightly, drain, and wash again with cold water to remove the excess salt.

2 Place one leaf on a plate, vein side upward, and put 1 teaspoon of filling in the center of the leaf near the stem end. Fold the stem end, and then both sides of the leaf over the filling and roll into a cigar shape. Repeat until all the stuffing is used up; you will have some leaves left over.

3 Line the base of a saucepan with the spare leaves, to prevent sticking, and pack stuffed grape leaves in tight layers. Mix the oil with a generous ½ cup water, the sugar, and lemon juice, and pour over the stuffed leaves.

4 Cover the *dolmas* with a heatproof plate, to prevent them opening during cooking, and simmer for 1 hour or until tender, adding hot water as it becomes absorbed. Cool in the pan and serve cold with lemon wedges.

Stuffed Cabbage Leaves

ZEYTINYAGLI LAHANA DOLMASI

Although this may seem an unusual way of serving cabbage, it is really quite simple to prepare. It is a very good way of getting children to eat this nutritious vegetable because it is a tasty dish, but remember then to omit the chiles.

Serves 4

1 white or green cabbage, washed
1 quantity stuffing, without mint (see page 36)
Juice of 1 lemon
Salt and ground black pepper
Pinch of paprika or crushed dried red chile

PREPARATION TIME: **1 HOUR**
COOKING TIME: **40 MINUTES**

1 Cut out the stalk of the cabbage with a sharp knife to give a cone shape, sprinkle with salt and boil rapidly for about 10 minutes in salted water. Once cooled, separate the leaves without tearing. Remove the tough central veins and cut the leaves into hand-size pieces.

2 Line the base of a saucepan with the thick pieces. Place one leaf on a plate, vein side upward, and place 1 teaspoon of filling in the center, toward the wider end. Fold the sides over the filling and roll the leaf into a cigar shape. Repeat until all the filling is used up; you will have some leaves left over.

3 Arrange the dolmas tightly in the saucepan and cover with a couple of leftover leaves, to prevent leaves coming undone during cooking. Add enough water to cover, bring to a boil, then add the lemon juice, seasoning, and paprika or crushed chile. Simmer for at least 40 minutes, until tender, adding hot water as it becomes absorbed. Cool in the saucepan before serving.

Tip

Choose a cabbage with fresh, crisp leaves. Loosely wrapped, it will keep well in the refrigerator for at least one week

Mussel Casserole

MIDYE PILAKI

This is a very popular dish in Turkish cuisine. It has a flavor the Turks enjoyed in their Mediterranean empire, where seafood was one of the most accessible and nutritious ingredients.

Serves 4

32 mussels, shelled
Olive oil, for shallow frying
1 onion, chopped
1 carrot, sliced
2 potatoes, peeled and diced
1 celery root, peeled and diced
2 fresh tomatoes, chopped rough
2 garlic cloves, crushed
Salt and ground black pepper
Juice of 1 lemon
Chopped fresh parsley,
    to garnish

PREPARATION TIME: **15 MINUTES**
COOKING TIME: **35 MINUTES**

1 Wash the mussels and cut the beards with a sharp knife.

2 Heat the oil in a pan and cook the onions until transparent. Add the carrot, potato, celery root, tomatoes, and garlic. Stir-fry for 1 minute, then add a generous ½ cup water. Cover and cook over medium heat for 15 minutes.

3 Add the mussels and cook for 10 minutes more. Season, add the lemon juice, and simmer for 5 minutes. Place in a warm serving dish, garnish with parsley, and serve.

Stuffed Mussels

MIDYE DOLMA

This special dish would be one of the dishes served at the table of many households during any celebratory dinner in Turkey.

Serves 4

½ cup long grain rice, washed and drained

1 Tbsp pine nuts

1 Tbsp raisins, washed and drained

1 onion, chopped

Generous ½ cup olive oil , plus a little extra to glaze

1 tsp sugar

1 tsp dried mint

Salt and ground black pepper

24 large mussels in the shell

Chopped fresh parsley, to garnish

PREPARATION TIME: **40 MINUTES**
COOKING TIME: **30 MINUTES**

1 Mix all the ingredients, except the mussels and parsley, together to make a raw stuffing.

2 Clean the mussels, scraping with a knife. Half open the round part of the shells and, with a pair of kitchen scissors, cut out the beards.

3 Stuff the empty half of the shells with the rice filling and tie a piece of string around each shell to keep them closed.

4 Place the shells in a saucepan with just enough water to cover. Bring to a boil, cover, and simmer for 30 minutes, until the water is absorbed.

5 When cooked, arrange the mussels in layers in a serving dish, cut the strings and brush with a little olive oil. Serve hot, garnished with parsley.

Fried Mussels

MIDYE TAVA

In this delicate dish, mussels are fried in a simple batter and served with lemon juice squeezed over.

Serves 4

32 shelled mussels

1 sachet (¼ oz) dried yeast

1¼ cups flour

2 eggs, separated

2 Tbsp margarine, melted

1 tsp salt

Olive oil, for shallow frying

Juice of 1 lemon

PREPARATION TIME: **25 MINUTES**
COOKING TIME: **25 MINUTES**

1 Wash the mussels thoroughly, clean off the edges, and dry.

2 In a large mixing bowl, soak the yeast in 2 tablespoons warm water for 10 minutes. Add 1 cup of the flour, the egg yolks, and melted margarine to the yeast mixture and mix well.

3 Whisk the egg whites with the salt, until quite stiff, then fold into the flour paste.

4 Heat some oil in a skillet. Dip the mussels first in the remaining flour, then into the batter, then fry until golden brown. Place in a serving dish lined with paper towels to absorb the excess oil. Drizzle the lemon juice over the mussels and serve.

Tip

When using fresh mussels, check them over carefully and discard any that are open before cooking. They could cause a stomach upset.

Meat and Poultry Dishes

ET YEMEKLERI
VE BEYAZ
ETLER

Lamb Casserole

KUZU GUVEC

Make sure you have plenty of bread to serve with this dish, to mop up the delicious juices.

Serves 6

1 Tbsp butter or margarine

2 lb tender lamb, diced

2½ cups meat stock

1 Tbsp tomato paste

12 shallots, peeled

1 garlic clove, crushed

6 cherry tomatoes

2 red bell peppers, seeded and quartered lengthwise

1 tsp dried or 1 Tbsp chopped fresh thyme

Salt and ground black pepper

Crusty bread, to serve

PREPARATION TIME: **20 MINUTES**
COOKING TIME: **1 HOUR 35 MINUTES**

1 Melt the butter or margarine in a saucepan and add the meat. Fry over high heat for 2 minutes to seal in the juices. Pour the stock over, stir in the tomato paste, and bring to a boil.

2 Add the shallots, garlic, tomatoes, and bell peppers. Mix well then add the herbs and seasoning.

3 Cover and cook over low heat (or in a preheated 350°F oven) for 1½ hours, or until the meat is tender and the stock reduced by half. Serve with chunks of warmed bread.

Eggplant Stew

PATLICANLI KEBAP

This is a very pretty stew. The word kebap *in Turkish means that the meat and the eggplants are browned in the skillet, sealing in the juices.*

Serves 4

4 small eggplants
2 Tbsp olive oil
8 shallots
1 red and 1 green bell pepper,
seeded and cut in chunks
1 hot chile, seeded and chopped
(optional)
1 lb mutton
1 Tbsp margarine
1 Tbsp tomato paste
2½ cups meat stock or water
Salt and ground black pepper
Parsley sprigs, to garnish

PREPARATION TIME: **15 MINUTES**
COOKING TIME: **2 HOURS**

1 Cut each eggplant lengthwise into four pieces and soak in salted water for 20 minutes. Drain and squeeze lightly to extract the excess water.

2 Heat the oil in a skillet and fry the eggplants lightly, in batches. Set aside when done.

3 In the same oil, fry the shallots, bell peppers, chile, if using, and the meat in the same way as the eggplants. Drain and set aside.

4 Melt the margarine in an ovenproof casserole, stir in the tomato paste, then pour in the stock. Bring to a boil, add the meat and vegetables, and season to taste. Cover and cook over low heat for 1½ hours (or alternatively in a preheated 350°F oven). Serve hot, garnished with parsley sprigs.

Burgers

KOFTE

These basic kofte could not be simpler to make. Just mix all the ingredients together, form into patties, and broil. Alternatively, you can cook them over a barbecue. Serve with French fries and hot pepper sauce, if you like.

Serves 4

1 lb ground beef or lamb

1 onion, chopped fine

2 Tbsp fresh bread crumbs

2 Tbsp chopped fresh parsley

1 tsp ground cumin (optional)

1 egg

Salt and ground black pepper

Olive oil, for brushing

PREPARATION TIME: **30 MINUTES**
COOKING TIME: **25 MINUTES**

1 Mix all the ingredients together in a large bowl with seasoning to taste. Knead thoroughly.

2 Preheat a hot broiler. Take walnut-size pieces in your hand and flatten to an oval shape. Continue making little patties until you have used up all the mixture.

3 Brush the broiler with a little oil and cook the burgers, turning them for even cooking. Serve hot.

Hasan Pasha Burgers

HASAN PASA KOFTE

These burgers call for twice-ground meat. Ask your butcher to do this for you, or pass the meat through a grinder, or whiz in a blender or food processor at home.

Serves 4

1 lb ground lamb or beef, ground again

½ cup fresh bread crumbs

1 onion, chopped fine

3 eggs

1 Tbsp butter

3 potatoes

1 Tbsp milk

Salt and ground black pepper

1 Tbsp tomato paste

PREPARATION TIME: **20 MINUTES**
COOKING TIME: **1 HOUR 40 MINUTES**

1 Preheat a 375°F oven. Knead the ground meat in a bowl with the bread crumbs, onion, and two of the eggs, adding a little water if necessary.

2 When thoroughly mixed, take pieces the size of an egg and roll in your wet hands to give an oval shape. Make shallow indentations in the center of each burger. Place in a large ovenproof dish with half of the butter. Cook in the oven for 25 minutes. When cooked, remove from the oven but leave the oven on.

3 Meanwhile, peel and chop the potatoes and boil in plenty of water. Once cooked, drain and mash.

4 Mix the mashed potato, milk, remaining egg, seasoning, and the remaining butter together and place in a saucepan. Cover and cook for about 5 minutes.

5 Fill the indentations in the burgers with the potato mixture. Mix the tomato paste with a little water and pour over the burgers. Place in the oven again for 25 minutes more.

Ladies' Thigh Burgers

KADIN BUDU KOFTE

This kofte *is equally good when chilled before serving, making it ideal picnic fare. Its English title is an exact translation from the sixteenth-century Turkish name. I hope you are happy with it!*

Serves 4

1 lb medium lean ground lamb
   or beef
1 onion, chopped fine
1 Tbsp butter
Generous ¼ cup long grain rice
1 Tbsp chopped fresh parsley
5 eggs
Salt and ground black pepper
1 Tbsp bread crumbs
Olive oil, for shallow frying

PREPARATION TIME: **20 MINUTES**
COOKING TIME: **1 HOUR**

1 Place two-thirds of the ground meat, the onion, and butter in a skillet and cook until the meat absorbs its own juice.

2 Wash the rice and boil in plenty of water until soft. Drain and set aside.

3 Combine the cooked meat mixture with the remaining raw meat and add the drained rice, parsley, three of the eggs, and salt and pepper. Knead thoroughly, break into pieces the size of a half lemon, and press into an oval shape. Place on a plate, covering each one with bread crumbs.

4 Whisk the remaining eggs in a bowl big enough to dip the burgers into. Heat some oil in a skillet and, when hot, dip each burger in the egg then fry on both sides until cooked through.

Beef with Navy Beans

ETLI KURU FASULYE

The aroma when cooking this dish is very appetizing and the meal itself very satisfying—it is a good one for cold winter evenings. Serve it hot with Rice with Noodles (on page 78).

Serves 4

1 lb navy beans
1 Tbsp butter
1 onion, chopped
1 lb chuck, cubed
3 fresh tomatoes, chopped
1 Tbsp tomato paste
5 cups beef stock or water
1 tsp crushed dried chile
   (optional)
1 tsp paprika
Salt and ground black pepper
Boiled rice, to serve

PREPARATION TIME: **OVERNIGHT PLUS 15 MINUTES**
COOKING TIME: **1 HOUR**

1 Soak the beans overnight.

2 The next day, melt the butter and fry the onion until transparent. Add the beef and cook for a few minutes. Then add the tomatoes with the tomato paste.

3 Pour in the stock and bring to a boil. Add the drained beans, crushed chile, if using, the paprika, and seasoning. Cover and cook over medium heat for 1 hour, or until the beans are tender, adding a little more hot water if necessary. Serve hot on a bed of rice.

Doner Kabob

DONER KEBAP

This is the closest you can get to eating an authentic doner kebap at home. Even in Turkey, many people will go out to eat it in a kebap restaurant. The meat should be tender and, ideally, marinated, and cooked slowly by the upright grill, and then cut into slices. It is traditionally placed on a bed of special bread, called pide, *and served with a tomato and a butter sauce. The best alternative bread to use is pita bread or ciabatta bread.*

Serves 4

FOR THE MARINADE

1 Tbsp olive oil

2 tsp plain yogurt

1 Tbsp tomato paste

2 bay leaves

A few fresh oregano leaves

Salt and ground black pepper

1 lb lamb, diced very fine

1 Tbsp butter

2 pita breads or small
   ciabatta loaves

1 Tbsp tomato paste

2 fresh tomatoes, skinned and
   chopped

Salt and ground black pepper

1 tsp paprika or crushed
   dried chiles

Scant 1 cup plain yogurt

PREPARATION TIME: **10 MINUTES PLUS OVERNIGHT**
COOKING TIME: **30 MINUTES**

Tip

To skin a tomato, first plunge it into a bowl of boiling water for 1 to 2 minutes and then into a bowl of cold water. The skin will split and you will be able to remove it easily with your fingers.

1 Mix the marinade ingredients in a large bowl and place the lamb pieces in, making sure that they are covered. Cover and chill overnight.

2 The next day, melt half the butter in a skillet and brown the lamb pieces.

3 Warm the bread under a broiler and cut into bite-size pieces. Place on warmed serving plates then spoon the meat over.

4 Mix the tomato paste with about 1¼ cups water and bring to a boil over medium heat. Add the chopped tomatoes and seasoning to taste. Cook until softened. In a separate pan, heat the remaining butter and paprika or chile.

5 Pour the tomato sauce over the lamb on the plates. Place a spoonful of yogurt on the side of each plate, then pour the butter sauce over, and serve hot with pickled chiles.

Grilled Lamb on a Skewer

SIS KEBAP

Sis kebap is a very traditional Turkish dish, as popular now as it was with the Nomadic Turkic tribes, from whom this method of cooking meat over an open fire came. Serve hot with eggplant salad and rice.

Serves 4

FOR THE MARINADE
2 large, fresh tomatoes, chopped
2 Tbsp olive oil
2 tsp dried oregano
1 tsp paprika
1 bouquet garni
Salt and ground black pepper

1 lb lamb, cubed
7 oz baby mushrooms
1 red or green bell pepper, seeded and cubed
8 bay leaves

PREPARATION TIME: **OVERNIGHT PLUS 15 MINUTES**
COOKING TIME: **30 MINUTES**

1 Mix the marinade ingredients in a large bowl and add the lamb. Stir to coat, then cover, and leave to marinate for at least 6 hours or overnight in the refrigerator.

2 The next day, preheat a hot broiler. Arrange the marinated lamb, mushrooms, bell pepper, and bay leaves on eight skewers, alternating the different components.

3 Broil, turning frequently, and brushing with the marinade from time to time. Serve hot, with Rice with Tomatoes (see page 78) and Eggplant Salad (see page 24).

Okra Casserole

ETLI BAMYA

The combination of green okra with the red tomatoes makes this dish very pretty. Try to buy small okra, as they are easier to cook and taste better.

Serves 4

1 lb okra
Juice of 1½ lemons
¼ stick butter
1 onion, chopped fine
8 oz stewing lamb or chuck beef
4 fresh plum tomatoes, skinned
Salt and ground black pepper

PREPARATION TIME: **30 MINUTES**
COOKING TIME: **1 HOUR**

1 Cut the stalk out of each okra, leaving a cone-shape indentation. Wash and soak the okra in a bowl filled with cold water and one third of the lemon juice for 1 hour.

2 Melt the butter in a saucepan and fry the onions and meat over medium heat. Add the tomatoes, reduce the heat, and simmer for 5 minutes.

3 Wash the okra again before adding to the casserole. Pour just enough water to cover, then cook for about 40 minutes.

4 Add seasoning and the remaining lemon juice, and simmer for 10 minutes more. Serve hot with rice pilaf.

Eggplant Moussaka

PATLICAN MUSAKKA

You can cook this dish using zucchini or potatoes if you prefer. Cook exactly the same way, but for zucchini moussaka add some fresh dill weed. Omit the meat for a vegetarian version.

Serves 4

4 small eggplants

Olive oil, for shallow frying

1 Tbsp margarine

1 onion, chopped

2 fresh ripe tomatoes, skinned
   and chopped

8 oz ground lamb or beef

Chopped fresh parsley,
   to garnish

PREPARATION TIME: **15 MINUTES**
COOKING TIME: **50 MINUTES**

1 Wash the eggplants, peel the skins horizontally in stripes, then slice in circles. Fry the eggplants in a little oil until they change color. Place in an ovenproof dish.

2 Preheat a 375°F oven. Heat the margarine in a saucepan, and add the onions, tomatoes, and ground meat. Cover and cook for 10 minutes over medium heat.

3 Pour the meat mixture over the eggplants. Add enough water to cover then cook in the oven for 40 minutes. Serve with chopped parsley scattered over.

Vegetable Casserole

TURLU

Use summer vegetables for a summer casserole or winter ones for a heartier winter stew. You can also use either lamb or beef or simply omit the meat altogether for a vegetarian dish.

Serves 4

2 potatoes, peeled
6 cherry tomatoes
1 carrot, peeled
1 eggplant
1 leek
1 red or green bell pepper, seeded
1 zucchini
¼ stick butter
8 oz chuck beef
1 onion, chopped
2½ cups beef stock or water
1 tsp dried oregano
Salt and ground black pepper
Warmed bread rolls, to serve

PREPARATION TIME: **20 MINUTES**
COOKING TIME: **40 MINUTES**

1 Chop the potatoes, tomatoes, carrot, eggplant, leek, bell pepper, and zucchini.

2 Heat the butter in a large saucepan. Add the meat and onion, and cook for 10 minutes.

3 Add the prepared vegetables, the stock, and the oregano. Cover and cook over medium heat for 30 minutes. When cooked, season to taste then serve with warmed bread rolls.

Stuffed Eggplant

PATLICAN KARNIYARIK

Such a very simple dish to make, with such delicious results. Serve hot with rice pilaf or hot crusty bread.

Serves 2

1 eggplant
Olive oil, for frying
1 Tbsp butter or margarine
7 oz ground beef or lamb
1 onion, chopped
1 Tbsp fresh chopped parsley
1 tsp tomato paste
Salt and ground black pepper
1 tomato, sliced into thin rings

PREPARATION TIME: **30 MINUTES**
COOKING TIME: **30 MINUTES**

1 Peel the skin of the eggplant in stripes. Cut in half lengthwise and scoop out the flesh without breaking the skin. The eggplant halves should look like two boats.

2 Heat a little olive oil in a skillet and fry the eggplants on all sides until lightly browned. Drain and place in a roasting pan, hollow sides up.

3 Preheat a 375°F oven. Melt the butter or margarine in a separate pan and cook the meat, onion, parsley, and tomato paste together.

4 When cooked, fill the eggplant shells with the meat mixture and place a few tomato rings on each one. Pour 1¼ cups water into the roasting pan. Cook in the oven for 30 minutes, or until the eggplants are cooked. Serve with rice.

Meat Stuffing for Vegetables

ETLI DOLMA ICI

Just as cold stuffed vegetables are popular appetizers, so hot stuffed vegetable dishes are widely offered as a main course. They are quite time consuming to prepare but among them are some of the most delicious of Turkish dishes. Serve with plain yogurt. The stuffing remains the same with any vegetable so I am giving the basic recipe for stuffing first.

Serves 4

1 lb ground beef or lamb

1 large onion, chopped fine

2 Tbsp rice, washed

3 Tbsp chopped fresh parsley

1 Tbsp chopped fresh dill weed (optional)

Salt and ground black pepper

1 Tbsp tomato paste

PREPARATION TIME: **15 MINUTES**

1 In a large bowl knead the ground beef or lamb with the onion, rice, herbs, and seasoning.

2 Mix the tomato paste with 3 tablespoons water and add to the meat mixture. Mix again until thoroughly combined.

Stuffed Tomatoes

DOMATES DOLMA

Another favorite in Turkish households, this dish could include bell peppers, stuffed exactly the same way as the tomatoes, to make a fine presentation of color and shape. The cooking time is approximate, depending on the firmness of the tomato used. A firm one is better, but simply reduce the cooking time if the tomato is soft as the tomatoes need to stay intact.

Serves 4

2 lb large tomatoes

1 quantity stuffing (see above and page 36)

1 Tbsp butter

1 tsp sugar

PREPARATION TIME: **40 MINUTES**
COOKING TIME: **30 MINUTES**

1 Wash the tomatoes. Cut off the tops with a sharp knife and set aside. Then scoop out the flesh with a teaspoon, being careful not to break the skin, and set aside.

2 Fill each tomato with stuffing and pack firmly in a large saucepan. Cover each one with its own top and pour in 2½ cups water. Add the butter, sugar, and the reserved flesh.

3 Cover and cook for 30 minutes. Serve with garlic or simply plain yogurt.

Stuffed Tomatoes ▶

Stuffed Zucchini

ETLI KABAK DOLMA

When you are out shopping for zucchini look for plump ones which are easier to hollow out. Keep the scooped out flesh, covered, in the refrigerator, to use the next day for Fried Zucchini (below).

Serves 4

4 zucchini

1 quantity stuffing (pages 36 or 54)

1 tomato, sliced horizontally

1 tsp tomato paste

1 Tbsp butter

Garlic yogurt, to serve

PREPARATION TIME: **40 MINUTES**
COOKING TIME: **40 MINUTES**

1 Wash the zucchini then cut them in half lengthwise. With a teaspoon, scoop the flesh out from inside without tearing the skin.

2 Fill each zucchini half quite tightly with the stuffing. Place a tomato ring on each one and pack them firmly in a suitable sized saucepan to prevent them moving while cooking.

3 Add enough water to cover the vegetables, stir in the tomato paste and butter, cover, and cook for 25 minutes over medium heat. Serve hot with garlic yogurt.

Fried Zucchini

KABAK MUCVERI

If you prepared the Stuffed Zucchini above and kept the scooped out flesh, use it in this recipe, making up the quantity as necessary.

Tip

To make garlic yogurt: peel and mince one garlic clove with a little salt. In a bowl, stir the garlic into 1 cup Greek-style yogurt and serve chilled.

Serves 4

1 Tbsp rice, washed

1 lb zucchini, peeled and shredded

1 Tbsp flour

2 Tbsp chopped fresh dill weed

2 Tbsp chopped fresh parsley

Salt and ground black pepper

3 eggs

Olive oil, for shallow frying

PREPARATION TIME: **40 MINUTES**
COOKING TIME: **30 MINUTES**

1 Boil the rice in water until soft, drain, and mix with the shredded zucchini in a large bowl. Add the flour, dill weed, parsley, and salt and pepper.

2 Beat the eggs, add to the zucchini mixture, and mix well.

3 Heat the oil in a skillet. Put tablespoonfuls of the mixture into the pan and fry on both sides.

4 As the patties are cooked, remove them to a serving dish lined with paper towels to absorb the excess fat. Serve hot.

Fried Zucchini ▶

Ankara Lamb Roast

ANKARA TAVA

This traditional Turkish meal would often be served when the whole family comes together on vacation. Serve it hot with baby potatoes.

Serves 4

1 Tbsp butter

2 lb boned leg of lamb, cut into 4 pieces

5 cups water or meat stock

1 onion, chopped fine

1 carrot, peeled and diced

1 cup peas

2 cups plain yogurt

½ cup flour

Salt and ground black pepper

1 egg

1 tsp paprika

PREPARATION TIME: **20 MINUTES**
COOKING TIME: **1 HOUR**

1 Melt the butter in a pan and fry the lamb pieces until evenly browned. Add the water or stock, the onion, carrot, and peas, and bring to a boil. Cover and simmer for 30 minutes.

2 Preheat a 375°F oven. Transfer the lamb and vegetables to an ovenproof dish, reserving the cooking liquid. Mix 2½ cups of the liquid with the yogurt, flour, and seasoning to taste. Pour this sauce over the lamb and vegetables.

3 Beat the egg lightly and pour evenly over the dish. Bake in the oven for 15 minutes. Sprinkle with the paprika and serve.

Meat and Vegetable Casserole

COMLEK KEBABI

This kebap *is usually cooked in an earthenware casserole called a "Comlek," hence its name. If you are able to use one, cook very slowly in a slow oven for a few hours as this will intensify the flavor and soften the meat. If you are using beef, double the cooking time.*

◀ *Meat and Vegetable Casserole*

Serves 6

1 Tbsp butter

2 lb lamb or beef, diced

6 shallots, peeled

4 oz string beans, sliced

1 eggplant, cubed

2 potatoes, peeled and cubed

2 carrots, peeled and diced

6 cherry tomatoes

2 oz okra, stems removed

1 hot chile, seeded and chopped

1 green bell pepper, seeded and chopped

1 Tbsp chopped fresh dill weed

Salt and ground black pepper

PREPARATION TIME: **20 MINUTES**
COOKING TIME: **1½ HOURS**

1 Melt the butter in a heatproof casserole and add the meat.

2 Layer the prepared vegetables over the meat, season with salt and pepper, and scatter over the dill weed.

3 Add a generous ½ cup water to the casserole, cover, and cook over low heat for 1½ hours, or until the meat is tender.

Lamb Casserole Cooked in Paper

KAGIT KEBABI

Make sure you seal the waxed paper very carefully over the top of each package so they do not come apart in the oven.

Serves 6

2 Tbsp butter or margarine

2 lb lamb, diced

1 onion, chopped

1 carrot, peeled and diced

1 lb potatoes, peeled and diced

1 fresh tomato, skinned and chopped

1 cup peas

1 Tbsp tomato paste

1 Tbsp red wine vinegar

2 Tbsp chopped fresh dill weed

1 tsp dried thyme

Salt and ground black pepper

PREPARATION TIME: **15 MINUTES**
COOKING TIME: **40 MINUTES**

1 Melt the butter or margarine in a saucepan and brown the meat evenly. Add the onion and carrot, cover, and cook until the juices are absorbed.

2 Add the potatoes, tomato, peas, tomato paste dissolved in a little water, and the vinegar. Cook for a few minutes more. Then add a scant 1 cup water, cover, and cook over low heat for 1 hour.

3 Preheat a 375°F oven. Cut six generous size pieces of waxed paper. Place equal portions of the casserole in the center of each sheet. Sprinkle the herbs and seasoning over each one. Fold the sides of the papers over the top to make packages. Place the parcels on an ovenproof tray and sprinkle with a little water. Bake in the oven for 20 minutes. Serve in their packages.

Celery Casserole

ETLI KEREVIZ

This is a surprisingly simple and delicious casserole. The aroma of celery is fresh and appetizing.

Serves 2

1 Tbsp butter

1 onion, chopped fine

1 lb stewing lamb, cubed

1 small celery root, peeled and cut into chunks

1 carrot, peeled and chopped

1 Tbsp tomato paste

Juice of 1 lemon

Salt and ground black pepper

Chopped fresh parsley, to garnish

PREPARATION TIME: **15 MINUTES**
COOKING TIME: **25 MINUTES**

1 Melt the butter in a casserole and lightly brown the onion. Add the lamb, cover, and cook until the juices are absorbed, about 3 minutes.

2 Add the celery root, carrot, tomato paste, and lemon juice, along with 1¼ cups water. Stir thoroughly and season.

3 Cook over medium heat for 25 minutes, or until the celery root is soft but firm. Serve with chopped fresh parsley scattered over.

Lamb Casserole Cooked in Paper ▲

Beef Kabobs

ADANA KEBAP

*These are molded kabobs prepared
with ground beef. The beef needs
to be quite fatty, so they make an
economical yet tasty dish.*

Serves 6

2 lb fatty ground beef
2 small onions, chopped fine
4 Tbsp chopped fresh parsley
Salt and ground black pepper
Warmed pita breads, to serve

TO GARNISH

2 onions, sliced thin
1 garlic clove, crushed
2 Tbsp chopped fresh parsley
A few small tomatoes
3 green bell peppers, seeded and
cut into strips lengthwise

PREPARATION TIME: **30 MINUTES**
COOKING TIME: **45 MINUTES**

1 Place the ground beef in a large bowl with the onions, parsley, and seasoning. Knead thoroughly.

2 Preheat a hot broiler. Have ready several metal skewers. Take an egg-size piece of the beef mixture in wet hands, and shape it around a skewer, elongating it to a length of about 4 inches. Repeat the process with the remaining meat mixture.

3 Place the skewers in the broiler pan and broil until cooked through, turning the skewers to ensure even cooking on both sides.

4 Prepare the garnish by mixing the onions with the garlic and parsley. Then lightly broil the tomatoes and bell peppers.

5 Serve the beef skewers on warmed pita breads, garnished with the onion and parsley mixture, and with broiled tomatoes and bell peppers on the side.

Beef Ragoût

PAPAZ YAHNISI

This is a very easy dish to prepare. Use good-quality beef and make sure the cubes are about the same size so they cook at the same rate.

Serves 6

1 Tbsp butter

2 lb lean beef, cubed

1 lb shallots, peeled

3 garlic cloves, crushed

2 Tbsp red wine vinegar

1 tsp cinnamon

1 tsp allspice

Salt and ground black pepper

Warmed bread, to serve

PREPARATION TIME: **15 MINUTES**
COOKING TIME: **2 HOURS**

1 Melt the butter in a large heatproof casserole and cook the beef in its own juices, until browned all over.

2 Add the shallots, garlic, vinegar, spices, and seasoning. Pour over 3½ cups hot water, cover, and cook over low heat for about 2 hours, or until the meat is tender. Serve hot with warmed bread.

Chicken with Mushrooms

MANTARLI TAVUK

This is a very colorful dish suitable for a family meal and it is delicious served with crusty bread rolls and a green salad.

Serves 4

1 Tbsp butter or margarine

4 chicken quarters

1 onion, chopped

1 garlic clove, crushed

1 Tbsp flour

Generous 2 cups chicken stock

1 Tbsp tomato paste

Generous ½ cup dry white wine

1 bouquet garni

3 bay leaves

Salt and ground black pepper

1 red bell pepper, seeded and
   chopped

8 oz button mushrooms

PREPARATION TIME: **15 MINUTES**
COOKING TIME: 1½ **HOURS**

1 Melt the butter or margarine in a saucepan and fry the chicken portions until evenly browned. Add the onion and garlic, and fry for 2 minutes more, then stir in the flour.

2 Pour in the stock with the tomato paste. Mix well, then add the wine and the herbs. Season to taste, cover, and cook over low heat for 1 hour. Add the bell pepper and the mushrooms, and simmer for 15 minutes more before serving.

Poussin Ragoût

PILIC YAHNI

If you cannot get poussins, you could substitute Cornish game hens.

Serves 4

3 Tbsp margarine

4 poussins

6 tiny pearl onions, peeled

2 garlic cloves, crushed

2 large fresh tomatoes, chopped

1¼ cups chicken stock or water

4 oz wild mushrooms, wiped

Salt and ground black pepper

PREPARATION TIME: **10 MINUTES**
COOKING TIME: **1½ HOURS**

1 Heat the margarine in a saucepan and add the poussins. Sauté for about 8 minutes, then add the onions, garlic, and tomatoes, and fry together for a few minutes more.

2 Add the stock and bring to a boil. Cover and cook over low heat for 1 hour.

3 Add the mushrooms and seasoning, and cook for 20 minutes more. Serve hot on a bed of rice.

Topkapi Palace Chicken

TOPKAPI TAVUK

This dish was developed in the Topkapi Palace kitchens, and is a firm favorite with the Turkish people.

Serves 4

2 Tbsp butter
1 small fresh chicken, cut into portions
5 oz chicken livers, chopped
6 shallots, peeled and chopped
1 Tbsp raisins, washed
1 Tbsp pine nuts
5 cups chicken stock
Scant 1 cup long grain rice, washed and drained
Salt and ground black pepper

PREPARATION TIME: **20 MINUTES**
COOKING TIME: **50 MINUTES**

1 Melt half the butter in a skillet and sauté the chicken pieces until evenly browned. Stir in the liver, shallots, and raisins, and fry together for a few minutes more. Transfer to a casserole pot.

2 Melt the remaining butter in a saucepan and fry the pine nuts until colored. Drain and add to the casserole.

3 Pour in the stock and bring to a boil. Stir in the drained rice and the seasoning. Cover and cook for 30 minutes over medium heat until all the juice is absorbed and the chicken is tender.

Chicken Burgers

TAVUK KOFTE

These burgers are dipped in flour, egg, and then bread crumbs before frying, which gives them a lovely crisp texture.

Serves 6

2 Tbsp margarine
3 Tbsp flour
½ cup milk
1 cup shredded Cheddar cheese
3 egg yolks
Salt and ground black pepper
9 oz cooked chicken, cut into strips
Olive oil, for shallow frying

FOR THE COATING
1 cup flour
2 eggs
2 cups fresh bread crumbs

PREPARATION TIME: **20 MINUTES**
COOKING TIME: **35 MINUTES PLUS CHILLING TIME**

1 Heat the margarine in a saucepan and stir in the flour. Stirring constantly, gradually add the milk. Then, still stirring, add the cheese, egg yolks, and seasoning. Cook for 5 minutes, stirring all the time.

2 Turn off the heat and add the chicken. Mix well, then chill for 2 hours.

3 Heat the oil in a skillet. Sift the flour onto a plate, whisk the eggs in a good-size bowl, and spread the bread crumbs out on a second plate.

4 Take walnut-size pieces of the chicken mixture and form into patties. Dip first into the flour, then into the egg, and, finally, into the bread crumbs. Fry evenly, drain, and serve.

Fish Casserole
BALIK PILAKI

Shrimp Casserole
KARIDES GUVEC

Anchovy Rice
HAMSILI PILAV

Skewered Swordfish
KILIC SIS

Fried Turbot
KALKAN TAVA

Skewered Shrimp
KARIDES SIS

Bonito with Sauce
SOSLU PALAMUT

Sea Bass with Raki Sauce
RAKI SOSLU LEVREK

Fish with Onions and Tomatoes
SOGANLI DOMATESLI BALIK

Steamed Fish
BALIK BUGULAMA

Seafood   BALIK YEMEKLERI
Dishes

Fish Casserole

BALIK PILAKI

Fish is not known for its color, but this dish is different and works very well with any type of fish.

Serves 6

1 Tbsp olive oil

1 onion, chopped

1 garlic clove, crushed

1 Tbsp flour

2½ cups fish stock

2 lb fish fillets, such as sea bass or gray mullet

1 potato, peeled

2 carrots, peeled and chopped

2 fresh ripe tomatoes, skinned and chopped

2 bay leaves

Salt and ground black pepper

Juice of ½ lemon

Fresh chopped parsley, to garnish

PREPARATION TIME: **15 MINUTES**
COOKING TIME: **35 MINUTES**

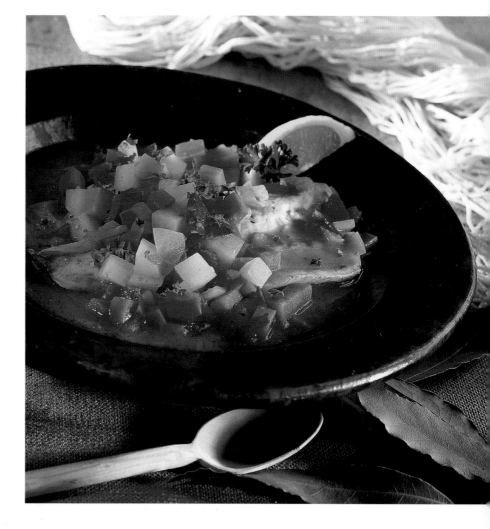

1 Heat the oil in a large saucepan and fry the onions and garlic for a few minutes.

2 Stir in the flour and pour in the stock. Bring to a boil, then add the fish, with the potato, carrot, tomato, and bay leaves. Season, cover, and simmer for 20 minutes, or until the potatoes are cooked.

3 Just before serving, sprinkle with lemon juice and parsley.

Shrimp Casserole

KARIDES GUVEC

This is a fine alternative way to eat fresh shrimp, and is often served, accompanied by chilled white wine, in scallop shells in seaside bars or small restaurants clustered at harborside.

Serves 4–6

2 lb fresh shrimp, shelled and cleaned
Salt and ground black pepper
2 Tbsp olive oil
1 Spanish onion, chopped
1 garlic clove, crushed
2 fresh tomatoes, skinned and chopped
1 green or red bell pepper, seeded and chopped
1 hot chile, seeded and chopped
1¼ cups shredded Cheddar cheese

PREPARATION TIME: **20 MINUTES**
COOKING TIME: **35 MINUTES**

1 Preheat a 425°F oven. Sprinkle the shrimp with a pinch of salt. Heat the oil in a saucepan and lightly brown the onion and garlic. Turn off the heat.

2 In a large bowl, mix the shrimp with the tomatoes, bell peppers, chile, and seasoning. Add the onion mixture.

3 Divide the mixture into portions, place in individual ovenproof dishes, and scatter over the Cheddar cheese.

4 Bake in the middle of the oven for 15 minutes, until cooked through and bubbling and golden on top.

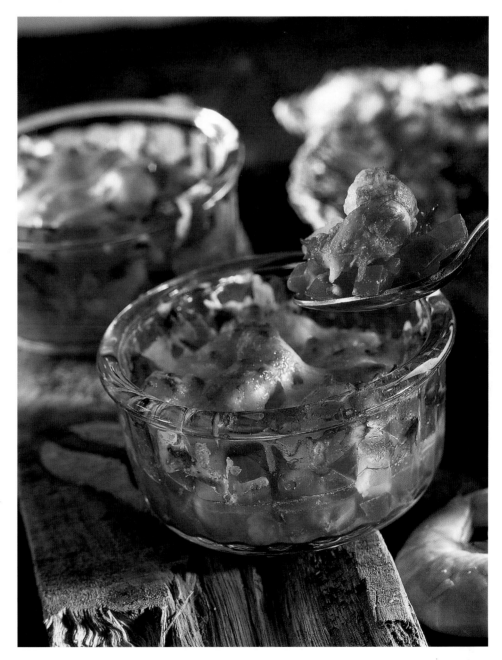

Anchovy Rice

HAMSILI PILAV

The people of the Black Sea region are famous for the ways they use fresh anchovies to create surprisingly delicious dishes. Even if you cannot find anchovies you can also use smelt which is widely available. The cleaning of this fish takes time but it is well worth the effort.

Serves 4

FOR THE PILAF
Generous 1¼ cups long grain rice
¼ stick butter
1¾ cups chicken stock

1 lb fresh anchovies
1 large Spanish onion, cut into rings
1 large fresh tomato, sliced horizontally
1 green or red bell pepper, sliced
Lemon wedges, to serve

PREPARATION TIME: **1 HOUR**
COOKING TIME: **1 HOUR**

1 Place the rice in a bowl and cover with hot water. Allow to cool, then drain, wash thoroughly, and drain again.

2 Melt the butter in a saucepan, add the stock, and bring to a boil. Add the rice, cover, and simmer for 5 minutes. Then reduce the heat and simmer for 15 minutes more, or until the liquid is completely absorbed.

3 Preheat a 350°F oven. Wash the fish under cold running water and separate the bones by cutting the side of the fish halfway through from the head and pulling the bone out.

4 Line a large ovenproof dish with half of the rice then place the onion and half the fish on top. Cover with the rest of the rice, fish, and tomato and bell pepper slices in layers.

5 Cook in the oven for 20 minutes. Serve hot, with lemon wedges for squeezing over.

Skewered Swordfish

KILIC SIS

Tasty and elegant, this dish is suitable for a small dinner party. The fish will remain intact during cooking and the flavor is very subtle. Serve hot with crusty white bread.

Serves 4

FOR THE MARINADE
1 Tbsp olive oil
1 Tbsp lemon juice
1 Tbsp salt
1 tsp paprika
6 bay leaves
Ground black pepper

1 lb swordfish, washed and cut into chunks
1 red onion, peeled and cut into chunks
1 green bell pepper, cut into bite-size pieces
Green salad leaves, to serve
Juice of 1 lemon, for sprinkling
A few radishes, to garnish

PREPARATION TIME: **30 MINUTES PLUS OVERNIGHT**
COOKING TIME: **20 MINUTES**

1 Mix the marinade ingredients together in a bowl large enough to accommodate the swordfish pieces. Add the fish and leave, covered, in the refrigerator for at least 6 hours.

2 Preheat a hot broiler. Thread the fish, onion, and bell pepper pieces onto metal skewers alternately. Broil for 5 minutes on each side, brushing occasionally with the marinade mixture.

3 Serve hot, on a bed of lettuce leaves, sprinkled with lemon juice, and garnished with radishes.

Fried Turbot

KALKAN TAVA

This is a very delicious fish which certainly does not require serving with a sauce. It is absolutely well worth getting if you can find it fresh. When it is simply fried and served with a crisp green salad it will make a lovely Sunday lunch.

Serves 4

2 lb fresh turbot

1¼ cups olive oil

½ cup flour

Salt and ground black pepper

Juice of 1 lemon

2 Tbsp chopped fresh parsley

PREPARATION TIME: **20 MINUTES**
COOKING TIME: **30 MINUTES**

---

1 If the fish is whole, first cut it into portions, then wash the portions thoroughly.

2 About 20 minutes before serving, heat the oil in a large skillet and mix the flour and seasoning together on a plate.

3 Dip the fish portions into the flour, making sure they are coated all over. Shake off the excess and fry until golden brown, turning once. Drain and place the portions in a warmed serving dish. Serve hot with lemon juice and parsley scattered over.

Skewered Shrimp

KARIDES SIS

Dublin Bay prawns, Florida lobsterette or langoustine from France—or shrimp can be used for this dinner party dish. It is important not to overcook the fish.

Serves 4

20 or 24 fresh shrimp, shelled
Juice of ½ lemon
2 fresh tomatoes
1 green bell pepper
6 bay leaves
1 lemon, sliced into rings
Salt and ground black pepper
1 Tbsp olive oil
Mixed salad leaves and boiled
new potatoes, to serve

PREPARATION TIME: **30 MINUTES**
COOKING TIME: **20 MINUTES**

1 Wash and drain the shrimp, brush with lemon juice, and set aside.

2 Cut the tomatoes and bell pepper into bite-size pieces, and halve the bay leaves.

3 Preheat a hot broiler. Thread the shrimp, tomato, and bell pepper pieces, halved bay leaves, and lemon rings alternately onto four metal skewers.

4 Broil for 5 to 7 minutes on each side, brushing with the olive oil seasoned with salt and pepper. Serve hot with mixed salad leaves and boiled new potatoes.

Bonito with Sauce

SOSLU PALAMUT

You can use any big fish for this dish. The sauce transforms even the dullest. Serve it with a mixed leaf salad and warmed bread.

Serves 4

1 large fish
1 carrot, peeled and sliced
1 onion, chopped
½ a small celery root, peeled and sliced
4 bay leaves
Juice of ½ lemon
Salt and ground black pepper

FOR THE SAUCE
½ cup cornstarch
4 egg yolks
Juice of 1 lemon
Salt
1¼ sticks butter

PREPARATION TIME: **20 MINUTES**
COOKING TIME: **50 MINUTES**

1 Place the fish, carrot, onion, celery root, bay leaves, and lemon juice in a large saucepan. Add salt and pepper to taste.

2 Cover with a little water and bring to a boil. Simmer for 25 to 30 minutes, then arrange the fish in a warmed serving dish.

3 For the sauce, place the flour, egg yolks, and lemon juice in a saucepan over medium heat. Stirring slowly, gradually add 1¾ cups water. Mix thoroughly, add salt, and keep on stirring until the sauce thickens. Turn the heat off then add the butter, stirring until blended.

4 Pour the sauce over the fish and serve immediately.

Sea Bass with Raki Sauce

RAKI SOSLU LEVREK

Raki is a strong spirit distilled from grain in Turkey, and flavored with aniseed and other aromatics. If you cannot find it, substitute the French apéritif, Pernod.

Serves 4

¼ stick butter
1 Spanish onion, peeled and chopped
1 large fresh tomato, chopped
4 large sea bass or grouper steaks
4 Tbsp dry white wine
Salt and ground black pepper
2 Tbsp heavy cream
4 Tbsp *raki* or Pernod
Chopped fresh parsley and dill weed, to garnish

PREPARATION TIME: **10 MINUTES**
COOKING TIME: **45 MINUTES**

1 Melt the butter in a saucepan and fry the onion until soft.

2 Add the tomato and the fish steaks, and pour in water just to cover. Stir in the wine and seasoning. Bring to a boil, cover, and cook over low heat for 20 minutes. Then place the fish steaks in a warmed serving dish, leaving the stock in the saucepan.

3 Heat the stock and stir in the heavy cream and *raki* or Pernod. Pour the sauce over the fish and serve garnished with the parsley and dill.

Sea Bass with Raki Sauce ▲

Fish with Onions and Tomatoes

SOGANLI DOMATESLI

BALIK

This is a very easy dish to make and tastes delicious.

Serves 4

1 lb red mullet or mackerel

1 Tbsp olive oil

2 onions, sliced into rings

4 fresh tomatoes, skinned

1 lemon, sliced

4 bay leaves

Salt and ground black pepper

Boiled new potatoes, to serve

PREPARATION TIME: **15 MINUTES**
COOKING TIME: **45 MINUTES**

1 Preheat a 375°F oven. Arrange the fish carefully in a large ovenproof dish.

2 Heat the olive oil in a skillet and fry the onions and tomatoes gently for a few minutes. Pour over the fish with enough water to cover.

3 Place the lemon rings and the bay leaves on top of the onion mixture, season, and cook in the oven for 30 minutes. Serve hot with boiled new potatoes.

Steamed Fish

BALIK BUGULAMA

Sardines and anchovies combine to produce a delicate flavor that tastes wonderful with new potatoes and butter.

Serves 4

2 lb fresh sardines or anchovies

1 onion, chopped very fine

1 Tbsp chopped fresh dill weed

1 Tbsp chopped fresh parsley

Salt and ground black pepper

1¼ cups fish stock

Lemon wedges, to serve

PREPARATION TIME: **25 MINUTES**
COOKING TIME: **30 MINUTES**

1 Wash the fish and arrange in a large saucepan in alternate layers with the onion and herbs. Add seasoning to taste and pour in the stock.

2 Bring to a boil, cover, and simmer for 8 to 10 minutes. Serve with lemon wedges for squeezing over.

Rice and *Pasta* Dishes

PILAVLAR VE
MAKARNALAR

Rice with Noodles

SEHRIYELI PILAV

In Turkish cuisine, it is not unusual to serve a dish of rice combined with noodles. This is a very basic dish and is suitable for serving with just about any main course dish.

Serves 6

2¼ cups long grain rice, washed and drained
1 Tbsp butter
3½ cups chicken stock
1 Tbsp or a good handful of noodles
Salt and ground black pepper

PREPARATION TIME: **5 MINUTES**
COOKING TIME: **35 MINUTES**

1 Soak the rice in hand-hot water, allow to cool, then drain.

2 Heat the butter in a saucepan and add the chicken stock. When it is boiling, add the rice and noodles. Stir once, season, and cover. Cook over medium heat until the liquid is absorbed, reducing the heat for the last 5 minutes.

Pasta with Mushrooms

MANTARLI MAKARNA

Wild mushrooms are used in this dish. They are widely available in supermarkets but you could substitute common cultivated ones if you wish.

Serves 4

1¼ cups meat stock
7 oz wild mushrooms, wiped and chopped
1 Tbsp butter plus a little extra
Salt and ground black pepper
7 oz roast beef, chopped
1 small onion, chopped
2 fresh tomatoes, chopped
1 Tbsp tomato paste
9 oz spaghetti
2 oz Cheddar cheese, shredded

PREPARATION TIME: **15 MINUTES**
COOKING TIME: **1 HOUR 45 MINUTES**

1 Bring the meat stock to a boil and stir in the mushrooms, butter, and salt and pepper. Simmer for 10 minutes, remove the mushrooms from the pan, and set aside the mushrooms and the stock.

2 Heat a teaspoon of butter in a skillet and stir in the roast beef, onion, tomatoes, tomato paste, and the stock from the mushrooms. Cover and cook for 30 minutes, adding hot water when necessary.

3 Cook the pasta according to the package instructions, drain, then place in a large serving dish.

4 Add the mushrooms to the sauce, cook for 5 minutes more, then pour over the pasta with the shredded cheese. Serve immediately.

Sultan Resat Rice

SULTAN RESAT PILAVI

As the name suggests, this is a traditional Ottoman dish that has stood the test of time. In the Ottoman Empire, the Sultan's corps of soldiers, the Jannissaries, would have one huge cauldron especially for the pilaf. When they revolted, a not uncommon event, the first sign of the upheaval would be the overturned pilaf cauldron.

Serves 6

2¼ cups long grain rice, washed and drained

¼ stick butter

3½ cups chicken stock or water

8 oz ground beef or lamb

1 bread slice, crusts removed, crumbed

1 onion, chopped fine

1 Tbsp margarine

1 Tbsp tomato paste

Salt and ground black pepper

PREPARATION TIME: **15 MINUTES**
COOKING TIME: **1 HOUR 10 MINUTES**

1 Soak the rice in hand-hot water, allow to cool, and drain.

2 Heat the butter in a saucepan, pour in the stock, and bring to a boil. Add the rice, cover, and cook over medium heat for 15 minutes. Then reduce the heat and simmer for 10 minutes more, until the liquid is absorbed. Keep warm.

3 Knead the ground meat with the bread crumbs and onion. Take walnut-size pieces of the mixture and, with wet hands, roll into balls.

4 Heat the margarine in a skillet and fry the meatballs evenly. Add a generous cup water, stir in the tomato paste, and season to taste. Cover and cook until the meatballs are tender.

5 Place the rice in a serving dish, make hollow in the center, and pour in the meatballs and sauce.

Rice with Chicken Livers and Raisins

IC PILAV

This rice is usually prepared to eat with the poultry and is cooked with poultry liver. Chestnuts are also added to the dish when it is served at New Year celebrations.

Serves 6

½ cup pine nuts

Scant ½ cup raisins

1 Tbsp butter

4 oz chicken or turkey liver, chopped

2 fresh tomatoes, skinned and chopped

3½ cups chicken stock

2¼ cups long grain rice, washed and drained

Salt and ground black pepper

PREPARATION TIME: **20 MINUTES**
COOKING TIME: **50 MINUTES**

1 Wash the pine nuts and raisins then dry.

2 Heat half the butter in a small pan and fry the pine nuts until they change color. Add the raisins and the liver and cook for 3 minutes.

3 Heat the remaining butter in a saucepan and fry the tomatoes for 2 minutes, then pour in the stock, and bring to a boil.

4 Drain the chicken livers, pine nuts, and raisins, and transfer to the tomato mixture. Add the rice and seasoning to taste. Cover and cook over medium heat for 30 minutes, until the liquid is absorbed.

5 Allow to rest for 5 minutes over very low heat, before serving with a turkey or chicken dish.

Rice with Tomatoes

DOMATESLI PILAV

This is again one of the simplest ways of cooking rice but it tastes very good. It is served as a side dish with broiled or barbecued meat or sausages.

Serves 6

2¼ cups long grain rice, washed and drained

¼ stick butter

3 fresh ripe tomatoes, skinned and chopped

3½ cups chicken stock

1 tsp tomato paste

Salt and ground black pepper

PREPARATION TIME: **5 MINUTES**
COOKING TIME: **40 MINUTES**

1 Soak the rice in hand-hot water, allow to cool, and drain.

2 Heat the butter in a saucepan and fry the tomatoes for a few minutes. Pour the chicken stock over and bring to a boil.

3 Add the rice, stir in the tomato paste, and season to taste.

4 Cover and cook over medium heat for 15 minutes, then reduce the heat, and simmer for 10 minutes more, until the liquid is absorbed.

Rice with Shrimp

KARIDESLI PILAV

This pilav is a meal in itself, simple to make and very nutritious.

Serves 6

9 oz shelled shrimp, fresh or
frozen
1 Tbsp butter
3½ cups chicken stock or water
2¼ cups long grain rice, washed
and drained
Salt and ground black pepper
½ cup cooked peas
Chopped fresh parsley,
to garnish

PREPARATION TIME: **10 MINUTES**
COOKING TIME: **30 MINUTES**

1 If using fresh shrimp, boil in salted water with 1 tablespoon white wine vinegar for 3 minutes.

2 Melt the butter in a saucepan and pour in the stock. Bring to a boil and add the rice. Season, cover, and cook over medium heat until the liquid is absorbed, about 20 minutes.

3 Line a ring mold with plastic wrap and place half the shrimp in the base, then half the rice over the shrimp, then the peas, and the rice again. Finish off with a layer of shrimp and rice. Pack the ingredients firmly into the mold.

4 To serve, invert the mold onto a serving dish and garnish with parsley.

Istanbul-style Pilaf

ISTANBUL PILAV

When in Istanbul... This popular dish in that city is very filling, so it is best served by itself or with a lightly broiled chicken breast.

Serves 4

1 Tbsp butter
2¼ cups long grain rice, washed and drained
A pinch of saffron, crushed fine
3½ cups chicken stock
1 Tbsp blanched almonds
1¾ cups petit pois or young peas
2 chicken livers or 1 chicken breast, cooked and chopped
Salt and ground black pepper
1 Tbsp shelled pistachios

PREPARATION TIME: **20 MINUTES**
COOKING TIME: **1 HOUR**

1 Heat the butter in a saucepan and add the rice. Cook for 5 minutes, stirring constantly.

2 Soak the saffron in about 2 tablespoons boiling water for 5 minutes. Pour over the rice with the stock. Stir, then add the almonds, petit pois, chicken liver or breast, and seasoning.

3 Stir again, cover, and cook for about 30 minutes. When cooked, leave the pilaf to rest over very low heat for 5 minutes, stir in the pistachios, and serve.

Pasta with Yogurt

YOGURTLU MAKARNA

Use any type of pasta shape you like for this dish.

Serves 4

1 lb fresh or no pre-cook pasta
Salt and ground black pepper
A few drops of olive oil
1 Tbsp butter plus a little extra
1 onion, chopped
7 oz ground beef or lamb
Generous ½ cup plain yogurt
2 garlic cloves, crushed
1 tsp paprika
1 tsp dried mint

PREPARATION TIME: **15 MINUTES**
COOKING TIME: **30 MINUTES**

1 Place the pasta in a saucepan of boiling water, with a little salt and a few drops of olive oil to prevent sticking. Cook for 10 minutes, or until the pasta is tender, then drain.

2 Heat the butter in a skillet and stir in the onion and meat. Cook, stirring continuously, until the meat juices are absorbed. Season to taste.

3 Place one quarter of the pasta in the base of a serving dish. Cover with one third of the meat mixture. Repeat twice more, then end with a layer of pasta.

4 Mix the yogurt with garlic, and pour this over the pasta, spreading evenly. Heat a teaspoon of butter in a skillet, stir in the paprika, then pour over the pasta as well. Serve hot with the mint scattered over.

Bulgur Wheat Pilaf

BULGUR PILAVI

This is a very healthy dish and it tastes delicious. You can find bulgur wheat in health-food stores and some supermarkets. There are two types of wheat on sale now. One is very thin wheat which is used in salads, koftes, and some soups, and does not require cooking. For this recipe the thicker bulgur wheat is used.

Serves 4

¼ stick butter
1 onion, chopped fine
1 fresh tomato, chopped fine
1 mild chile or green bell pepper,
  chopped fine
1½ cups bulgur wheat
4½ cups hot chicken stock
  or water
1 Tbsp tomato paste
Salt and ground black pepper

PREPARATION TIME: **10 MINUTES**
COOKING TIME: **25 MINUTES**

1 Melt the butter in a saucepan and fry the onion until translucent. Add the tomato and chile or bell pepper, and, stirring continuously, cook for a few minutes.

2 Add the bulgur wheat, season, and stir over high heat for 1 minute.

3 Pour over the hot chicken stock or water, stir in the tomato paste, and season with salt and pepper. Cook over medium heat until the liquid is absorbed.

4 Allow to rest over very low heat for 5 minutes before serving.

Fresh Pasta Drops

MANTI

This is a very famous dish from the Black Sea region. It is actually quite similar to tortellini and is traditionally served with garlic yogurt and a dash of melted butter with paprika. It is a time-consuming dish but with absolutely wonderful results. Serve with a light appetizer because it is quite filling.

Serves 4

4 cups flour
1 large egg
Salt and ground black pepper
9 oz ground beef or lamb
1 onion, chopped fine
1 Tbsp chopped fresh parsley
Butter, for brushing
Hot beef stock or water

FOR THE SAUCE
2 cups plain yogurt
1 garlic clove, crushed
¼ stick butter
1 tsp paprika or crushed dried chile
1 tsp dried mint

PREPARATION TIME: **1 HOUR
PLUS 1 HOUR STANDING TIME**
COOKING TIME: **55 MINUTES**

1 Sift the flour and ½ teaspoon salt into a large bowl and make a hollow in the center. Knead with the egg, and sufficient water to a smooth, workable dough. Cover with a wet cloth and leave for 1 hour.

2 Sprinkle the work surface with flour and roll the dough out into a small circle. Gradually increasing the size of the circle, roll it as thin as possible to a thickness of ⅛ inch. Cut the pastry into 2-inch squares.

3 Preheat a 375°F oven. Mix together the ground meat, onion, parsley, and salt and pepper. Place 1 teaspoon of this mixture in the center of a pastry square. Bring the corners of the square together over the top of the filling and squeeze with your fingers to stick firmly. Repeat with the rest of the squares.

4 Arrange the packages in a deep ovenproof dish and brush with a little butter. Bake in the oven for 25 minutes, until lightly browned. Now pour over just enough hot stock or water to come halfway up the *manti*. Return to the oven and cook for about 30 minutes more, or until the liquid is absorbed. Place the *manti* in a warmed serving dish.

5 Mix the yogurt with garlic and pour over the pastries. In a small skillet, melt the butter and stir in the paprika or crushed chile. Stir for 1 minute then pour over the *manti* as well. Serve hot with dried mint scattered over.

Pasta with Leeks

PIRASALI MAKARNA

Leeks and bacon complement each other wonderfully in this delicious pasta bake.

Serves 4

9 oz tagliatelli

2 leeks, chopped

6 bacon slices, broiled

3 eggs

Generous 1 cup plain yogurt

Salt and ground black pepper

7 oz Cheddar cheese, shredded

PREPARATION TIME: **10 MINUTES**
COOKING TIME: **30 MINUTES**

1 Cook the pasta according to package instructions, then drain. Simmer the leeks in water until tender.

2 Preheat a 400°F oven. Line an ovenproof dish with the bacon, then place the pasta and the leeks in layers, finishing with a layer of pasta.

3 Whisk the eggs into the yogurt, and add salt and pepper. Spread over the pasta. Scatter the cheese evenly over the top. Cook in the oven for 25 minutes. Serve hot.

Pasta in the Oven

FIRINDA MAKARNA

The pasta used in this recipe is a specialty of the Black Sea region, and it is similar to spaghetti, but it is ⅛ inch in diameter. You can usually find it in good delicatessens, but spaghetti is a good substitute.

Serves 4

1 lb dried spaghetti

Salt and ground black pepper

A few drops of olive oil

2 Tbsp butter

7 oz Cheddar cheese, shredded

3 eggs

2½ cups milk

PREPARATION TIME: **5 MINUTES**
COOKING TIME: **1 HOUR**

1 Place the pasta in a saucepan of boiling water, with a little salt and a few drops of olive oil to prevent sticking. Cook for 15 minutes, or until the pasta is tender, then drain.

2 Preheat a 400°F oven. Place the pasta in a deep ovenproof dish and mix well with the butter and half the cheese. Scatter the remaining cheese on top.

3 Beat the eggs with the milk, and salt and pepper. Pour over the pasta, spreading evenly. Cook in the oven for 25 minutes. Cut into squares and serve hot.

Rose Pasta

GUL MANTI

These manti *are named for their appearance rather than the inclusion of rose water. They are a little awkward to make but look so attractive that the extra effort is worthwhile.*

Serves 4

6 oz ground beef or lamb

1 onion, chopped fine

½ cup chopped fresh parsley

Salt and ground black pepper

10 oz phyllo pastry, fresh or frozen

1 egg yolk, for brushing

Garlic yogurt, to serve

PREPARATION TIME: **1 HOUR**
COOKING TIME: **25 MINUTES**

1 Place the meat in a bowl with the onion, parsley, and seasoning. Mix well.

Tip

Phyllo pastry dries out very quickly and becomes unworkable. To prevent this, keep the pastry sheets under a damp dish towel, and only take out one at a time. Any leftover pastry can be rolled up, sealed in a freezer bag, and kept in the freezer.

2 Preheat a 350°F oven. On a floured surface, cut the phyllo pastry into large triangles. Place 1 tablespoon of the meat mixture in the center of one side of a triangle. Fold over the two corners and roll like a cigar. Then, starting from one end, roll the cigar shape into a rose shape, sticking the end with a little water. Repeat with all the triangles.

3 Brush the *manti* with egg yolk and bake in the oven for 25 minutes, until golden. Place in a serving dish and pour over the garlic yogurt.

Spinach Pie
ISPANAKLI BOREK

Cheese Pie
PEYNIRLI BOREK

Raw Pie
CIG BOREK

Cheese Rolls
PUACA

Puff Pie
PUF BOREK

Water Pie
SU BOREGI

Talas Pie
TALAS BOREK

Savory Pies BOREKLER

Spinach Pie

ISPANAKLI BOREK

This is a very good way to make children eat spinach. It is easy to make, especially if you use ready-made pastry. You can either use phyllo or puff pastry, but with phyllo pastry it is quite crispy.

Serves 4

¼ stick butter

1 onion, chopped fine

2 lb fresh spinach leaves, washed and chopped

Salt and ground black pepper

1 lb puff pastry

A little melted butter

10 oz feta cheese, cubed

1 egg yolk, for brushing

PREPARATION TIME: **30 MINUTES**
COOKING TIME: **45 MINUTES**

1 Melt the butter in a large skillet, fry the onions until soft, then add the spinach. (It may seem quite a lot to begin with but, once cooked, the spinach will reduce.) Cook for a few minutes, stir in seasoning to taste, drain, and set aside.

2 Preheat a 375°F oven. On a floured surface, roll out half the pastry as thin as possible to line a 12-inch square, deep ovenproof dish. Brush the dish with a little melted butter and sprinkle with flour. Line the dish with the pastry and fill first with the cheese cubes then with the spinach and onion mixture.

3 Roll out the remaining pastry to a square large enough to cover the dish, place over the filling, and seal the edges with a little water.

4 Brush the pie with half the egg yolk and cook in the oven for 25 minutes, until nicely browned. Remove from the oven, turn the pie over and brush again with the remaining egg yolk, then return to the oven for 20 minutes more. Serve hot.

Tip

If you like, add four or five cooked bacon slices for a different taste. You can also substitute canned spinach for the fresh, but drain it very thoroughly.

Cheese Pie

PEYNIRLI BOREK

Besides feta cheese, you could also use different ingredients for this pie. For example, cooked ground meat with herbs, or cooked chicken pieces in cream.

Serves 4

6 sheets phyllo pastry
1 Tbsp butter
1 Tbsp plain yogurt
2 eggs
1 lb feta cheese
1 cup chopped fresh parsley
1 tsp chili powder or paprika
Salt and ground black pepper

PREPARATION TIME: **30 MINUTES**
COOKING TIME: **25 MINUTES**

1 Preheat a 375°F oven. Grease an ovenproof dish, and line with one of the phyllo pastry sheets.

2 Mix the butter, eggs, and yogurt together in a bowl. Brush a little of this mixture onto the phyllo pastry. Place another sheet on top and brush with the mixture again, then repeat.

3 Mash the cheese in a separate bowl with the parsley, chili powder or paprika, and salt and pepper. Spread this mixture evenly over the pastry in the dish.

4 Sandwich the remaining pastry sheets with the egg mixture on top of the filling. Brush the top sheet as well, then cook in the oven for 25 to 30 minutes. Serve hot.

Raw Pie

CIG BOREK

This is a very light, crisp, and tasty borek. You may cook the ground meat beforehand if you do not want to use it raw.

Serves 4

9 oz ground beef or lamb
1 onion, chopped fine
1 tsp tomato paste
Salt and ground black pepper
2¼ cups flour
1 egg
Olive oil, for shallow frying

PREPARATION TIME: **1 HOUR**
COOKING TIME: **20 MINUTES**

1 Knead the ground meat in a bowl with the onion, tomato paste, and salt and pepper.

2 Sift the flour onto the work surface, make a well in the center, and break the egg into it. Add salt and knead to a medium-soft dough, adding a little water if necessary. Divide the dough into balls about half the size of a lemon, place a damp dish towel over the balls, and allow to rest for 20 minutes.

3 Roll each ball out to a 4-inch circle. Place 1 teaspoon of filling in one half of the circle, fold the other half over the top, and seal the edges with a little water. Heat the oil in a skillet and, when hot, fry the pastries evenly, turning once. Drain and serve hot.

Cheese Rolls

P U A C A

These little pastries can be made in advance as they keep well. They can be reheated the next day without losing their flavor.

Serves 4

Generous ½ cup margarine

1 egg

½ cup unsweetened yogurt

2 tsp baking powder

3 cups flour

9 oz feta cheese

½ cup chopped fresh parsley

1 tsp paprika

1 tsp ground black pepper

1 egg yolk

Sesame or poppy seeds, for
   sprinkling

PREPARATION TIME: **50 MINUTES**
COOKING TIME: **30 MINUTES**

---

1 Melt the margarine and, when cooled, beat with the egg, yogurt, and baking powder. Add the flour and knead to a soft dough.

2 Mash the cheese with the parsley, paprika, and black pepper.

3 Preheat a 400°F oven. Take walnut-size pieces of the pastry and, on a floured surface, flatten them into 2-inch circles. Place the filling on one half of a circle and fold the other half over the top to make a crescent shape. Cut round the edges of the shape with a cookie cutter to smooth the edges and seal. Repeat until all the pastry is used up.

4 Brush each roll with egg yolk and sprinkle with sesame or poppy seeds. Place on a greased cookie sheet and bake in the oven for 30 minutes, until golden.

Puff Pie

PUF BOREK

*There is a choice of fillings for
this* borek, *one is a meat-based
mixture and the other uses
feta cheese.*

Serves 6

2½ cups flour
1 Tbsp margarine
1 egg yolk
Salt
2 Tbsp butter, melted
Olive oil, for shallow frying

FOR THE MEAT FILLING
6 oz ground beef or lamb
2 onions, chopped fine
Salt and ground black pepper

FOR THE CHEESE FILLING
1 Tbsp margarine
8 oz feta cheese, mashed
1 egg white
1 cup chopped fresh parsley
Ground black pepper

PREPARATION TIME: **1 HOUR STANDING
TIME PLUS 45 MINUTES**
COOKING TIME: **25 MINUTES**

1 Sift the flour into a large bowl and knead with about ½ cup water, the egg yolk, margarine, and a little salt, to a soft, workable dough. Cover with a wet dish towel and set aside for 1 hour.

2 Divide the dough into six equal pieces and roll each one out to an 8-inch circle. Brush each circle with a little melted butter and place in a stack. Cover with a damp dish towel again and allow to stand for 1 hour more.

3 To prepare the meat filling, melt the margarine and fry the meat with the onions. Season with salt and pepper. For the cheese filling, mix the cheese with egg white, parsley, and pepper.

4 Roll a circle of dough as thin as possible. Place a spoonful of the filling on one half of the circle, then fold the other half over the top. Seal the edges with a little water. Repeat with the remaining circles.

5 Heat the oil in a large skillet and fry the pastries evenly. Drain and serve hot.

Water Pie

SU BOREGI

This is a very light and delicious pie with a crispness to it which comes from immersing the pastry in water. You can serve it as an appetizer, or as a dessert if you change the filling to jelly, lemon cheese, or mincemeat, dusted with confectioners' sugar.

Serves 6

4 cups flour

3 eggs

1 Tbsp salt

¾ cup cornstarch

6 Tbsp margarine

FOR THE FILLING

2 Tbsp margarine

1 large onion, chopped

7 oz ground lamb

Salt and ground black pepper

1 Tbsp chopped fresh parsley

PREPARATION TIME: 1½ **HOURS**
COOKING TIME: 1½ **HOURS**

1 Sift the flour into a bowl and make well in the center. Break the eggs into the well and mix the flour with the eggs, gradually adding ½ cup water and the salt. Knead to a soft dough, adding a little more water as necessary. Divide into nine pieces, one of them twice the size of the other eight. Flatten each piece and cover with damp dish towel. Allow to stand for 30 minutes.

2 Meanwhile, prepare the filling. Heat the margarine in a skillet and fry the onions until transparent. Add the ground lamb and season. Cover and cook over medium heat. Finally, stir in the fresh parsley and let cool slightly before using.

3 You will need a 9-inch round cookie sheet. On a floured board, roll the largest piece of dough to twice the size of the cookie sheet. Brush the cookie sheet with a little margarine and line with the largest piece of dough. Roll the rest of the dough pieces into 9-inch circles and place on top of each other, sprinkling cornstarch between each layer.

4 Have ready a large bowl of cold water. In a large pan, bring 4¼ quarts water to a boil, with 1 tablespoon salt, and immerse each circle individually in the boiling water for 1 minute. Drain each layer, dip in the cold water, and drain again.

5 Preheat a 375°F oven. Melt the margarine and place four of the circles in the cookie sheet, brushing between each layer with the margarine. Spread the filling evenly and repeat the same process with the remaining four dough circles. Fold the edges of the larger one over and seal with melted margarine.

6 Bake for 1½ hours. Carefully invert the borek onto a serving dish and serve hot.

Talas Pie

TALAS BOREK

The talas ici, *the stuffing for the Talas Pie, is quite time-consuming to make, so ensure you have plenty of time in which to prepare this dish. Make the pastry while the filling is cooking as it needs to rest before being used.*

Serves 6

3½ cups flour

1 Tbsp margarine

2 Tbsp water

1 tsp salt

¼ cup olive oil

1 egg yolk

FOR THE STUFFING

2 Tbsp margarine

2 onions, chopped

2 lb lean lamb, diced

1 Tbsp tomato paste

1 tsp dried thyme

Salt and ground black pepper

PREPARATION TIME: **1 HOUR 40 MINUTES**
COOKING TIME: **1½ HOURS STANDING TIME PLUS 30 MINUTES**

1 For the stuffing, melt the margarine in a saucepan and fry half the onion and the meat, until the meat juices are reabsorbed. Stir in the tomato paste and add 1¼ cups hot water. Bring to a boil and simmer for 1 hour. Add the remaining onion and simmer for 30 minutes more. Add the thyme and seasoning, mix well, and set aside until needed.

2 To make the pastry, sift the flour into a large bowl, add the margarine, water, and salt, and knead to a soft dough. Cover the dough with a wet dish towel and leave for 1 hour.

3 Roll out the dough to a ½-inch thick rectangle. Cut the pastry into 12 equal pieces and allow to stand for 15 minutes.

4 Preheat a 375°F oven. Now dip each piece of pastry in the olive oil and roll out as thin as possible. Place some meat filling in the center of each one and fold the corners over to make packages.

5 Sprinkle an ovenproof dish or roasting pan with water. Beat the egg yolk with 1 teaspoon of the olive oil and 1 tablespoon water, then brush the pastries. Bake in the oven for 30 minutes, until evenly browned.

Cookies
and
Cakes
BISKUVILER
VE KEKLER

Shortbread

UN KURABIYESI

This shortbread is so simple to make. Children will enjoy helping you to shape the cookies and press in the almonds.

Makes 16 cookies

1 cup flour
1 stick butter
⅓ cup rice flour
4 Tbsp sugar plus extra for
    sprinkling
16 whole blanched almonds

PREPARATION TIME: **30 MINUTES**
COOKING TIME: **30 MINUTES**

1 Preheat a 325°F oven and butter a cookie sheet. Blend the butter into the flour until the mixture resembles bread crumbs.

Add the rice flour and mix well. Stir in the sugar and knead to a smooth dough.

2 Break walnut-size pieces from the dough and flatten with your fingers, push an almond into the center of each one, and place on the cookie sheet.

3 Bake in the oven for 25 to 30 minutes, until pale brown in color. Sprinkle with a little sugar. Transfer the cookies to a wire rack to cool and store in an airtight container.

Cinnamon Cookies

TARCINLI KURABIYE

Crisp and aromatic cookies— delicious at coffee time. They keep well stored in an airtight container.

Makes 20 cookies

½ cup margarine
Generous ½ cup sugar
1¾ cups whole-wheat flour
1 egg
1 tsp ground cinnamon
20 whole blanched almonds

PREPARATION TIME: **30 MINUTES**
COOKING TIME: **25 MINUTES**

1 Preheat a 375°F oven. Butter a cookie sheet. Blend the margarine with the sugar until light. Beat the egg in a separate bowl with a little

of the flour. Add to the margarine mixture, little by little, and, when mixed, stir in the flour and cinnamon. Knead the dough lightly until smooth.

2 Break off walnut-size pieces of dough, flatten with a fork dipped in hot water, and press an almond into each cookie.

3 Place on the cookie sheet and bake in the oven for 25 minutes. Cool on a wire rack and store in an airtight container.

Cinnamon Cookies ▶

Raisin Cupcakes

UZUMLU KEK

This is a very easy cake mixture and gives good results every time. You can omit the raisins and use candied peel, glacé cherries, or a teaspoon of cocoa powder in their place. These cupcakes are baked in paper cases.

Makes about 15 cupcakes

½ cup margarine

Generous ½ cup sugar

2 eggs

1 cup self-rising flour

Scant 1 cup raisins

PREPARATION TIME: **10 MINUTES**
COOKING TIME: **25 MINUTES**

1 Preheat a 350°F oven. Blend the margarine with the sugar until light. Beat the eggs in a separate bowl with a little of the flour. Then, little by little, add to the margarine mixture, stirring all the time. Stir in the flour, then the raisins, and mix well.

2 Place 2 teaspoons of the mixture in a paper case. Repeat until all the mixture has been used up.

3 Bake the cupcakes in the oven for 20 to 25 minutes.

Orange Cake

PORTAKALLI KEK

The orange aroma is very intense and refreshing, and this lovely light tea-time cake is best eaten while fresh as it does not keep for long. Try serving it with a little whipped cream.

Makes a 1 lb loaf cake

½ cup margarine
Generous ½ cup sugar
1 Tbsp plain yogurt
2 eggs
1¼ cups self-rising flour
1 tsp baking soda
1 tsp shredded orange rind
1 Tbsp orange juice
Candied peel or orange slices,
to decorate

PREPARATION TIME: **20 MINUTES**
COOKING TIME: **1 HOUR**

1 Preheat a 180°F oven and grease a 1-pound loaf pan. Blend the margarine and sugar together until light. Add the yogurt.

2 Beat the eggs in a separate bowl with a little of the flour. Sift the rest of the flour with the baking soda and mix all the ingredients together.

3 Gradually add the eggs to the margarine mixture, stirring constantly. When mixed, add the flour. Finally add the orange zest.

4 Transfer the mixture to the loaf pan and bake in the oven for 1 hour. Transfer the cake to a wire rack and, while still hot, make a few skewer holes, and pour the orange juice over. Decorate with candied peel or orange slices.

Chocolate Cake

CUKULATALI PASTA

A cake for a special occasion. My chocolate cake is relatively easy to make with very good results, and the combination of pistachios and chocolate gives it a subtle, distinctive taste.

Makes an 8-inch sandwich cake

¾ cup margarine

Generous ¾ cup sugar

3 eggs

1¾ cups all-purpose flour

1 tsp baking powder

1 Tbsp cocoa powder

Shredded rind of 1 orange

Chocolate vermicelli or chocolate curls, to decorate

FOR THE FILLING

1¼ sticks butter, softened

1 Tbsp cocoa powder

2 cups confectioners' sugar, sifted

1 Tbsp orange liqueur (optional)

¼ cup pistachios, chopped (optional)

FOR THE FROSTING

Scant ½ cup confectioners' sugar, sifted

¼ cup cocoa powder

Generous ½ cup heavy cream

PREPARATION TIME: **1 HOUR**
COOKING TIME: **30 MINUTES**

1 Preheat a 375°F oven and grease and line two 8-inch round cake pans. Blend the margarine and sugar together until light. Add the eggs, one at a time, with a little flour. Beat thoroughly and stir in the cocoa powder and orange rind. Add the remaining flour and beat well.

2 Pour into the cake pans and bake in the oven for 25 to 30 minutes. Let the cakes cool slightly in the pans, then turn out onto a wire rack to cool completely.

3 To make the filling, combine the butter, cocoa powder, confectioners' sugar, and orange liqueur, if using, together in a mixing bowl and beat well until smooth and glossy. Fold in the pistachios, if using. Sandwich the cakes together with the filling.

4 For the frosting, mix the sifted icing sugar with the cocoa powder in a mixing bowl. Stir in 2 tablespoons hot water and beat well until smooth. Spread evenly over the top with a knife dipped in hot water. Whip the heavy cream until thick then spread around the sides of the cake with a fork. Decorate with chocolate vermicelli or curls.

Chocolate Mosaic Slices

MOZAYIK

This is a children's birthday party favorite in Turkey. It is very easy to make and, as it is frozen, keeps well. I make it with plain butter cookies which you can get from any good supermarket.

Makes about 20 slices

1 lb plain butter cookies
1 stick butter or margarine
2 Tbsp cocoa powder
2 Tbsp sugar
4 eggs

PREPARATION TIME: **30 MINUTES PLUS 4 HOURS' FREEZING TIME**

1 Break the cookies into crumbs by hand or with a rolling pin. Do not use a blender or food processor because you need small pieces, not powdered cookies.

2 Melt the butter or margarine in a pan with the cocoa powder. When cooled, add 2 tablespoons water.

3 Place the sugar and the eggs in a blender or food processor and blend until smooth. Transfer to a bowl, stir in the cocoa mixture, and then the cookie crumbs.

4 Place the mixture on a large piece of aluminum foil and roll it firmly into a cylinder shape. Freeze, wrapped in the foil, for 4 to 5 hours, then cut into slices, and serve. If you have some left over, wrap it in foil again and put it back in the freezer.

Tip

This recipe contains raw egg. Any woman who is, or suspects she is, pregnant should not eat it. Those with a weak immune system are also advised not to eat uncooked egg.

Desserts, Preserves, and Drinks

TATLILAR

Baklava

BAKLAVA

This is a simple-to-make version of the famous dessert. The baklava can be prepared using ready-made phyllo pastry—you will need 24 sheets—which reduces the preparation time considerably. However, I have given the ingredients for the dough if you would prefer to do it yourself. If you do, make sure you roll out the pastry sheets thinner than phyllo pastry.

Makes 24 pieces

FOR THE PASTRY
2 cups flour
2 eggs
1 tsp salt
1 Tbsp water
1 tsp olive oil
1⅓ cups cornstarch
1½ sticks sweet butter, melted

FOR THE FILLING
1½ sticks sweet butter
2 cups walnuts or pistachios, chopped fine
Generous ¼ cup light brown sugar

FOR THE SYRUP
1¼ cups sugar
1 Tbsp lemon juice

PREPARATION TIME: **15 MINUTES**
COOKING TIME: **30 MINUTES**

1 For the pastry, sift the flour and mix in the eggs, salt, and 1 tablespoon water. Knead for 15 minutes, cover with a damp dish towel, and leave for 1 hour to rise.

2 Meanwhile, prepare the filling. Mix the chopped nuts with sugar and spread this evenly over the pastry. Melt the butter and drizzle over the filling.

3 When the pastry dough has been standing for 1 hour, spread the olive oil over the dough, knead again, and leave for 15 minutes more.

4 Cut the dough into eight equal pieces and sprinkle each with cornstarch. Now roll each piece into a 6-inch circle, sprinkle with cornstarch, and place in a stack. Leave for 20 minutes. Then roll out the dough again, thinner than phyllo pastry, in rectangles. The layers of dough can be rolled out all together, but they should be alternated each time. Stack the pastry sheets and cut them exactly the same size as your cake pan.

5 Preheat a 425°F oven. Brush a 7- by 9-inch shallow cake pan with melted butter and place half the pastry sheets, brushing each one with butter, in the cake pan. Spread the filling evenly, then place the remaining sheets on top, brushing each with butter. Cut through all the layers of the pastry with a sharp knife to make six rectangles, then criss-cross each rectangle to create 24 triangular, bite-size shapes.

6 Bake in the oven for 15 minutes, then reduce the oven temperature to 350°F and bake for a further 15 minutes until the pastry is crisp and golden.

7 Meanwhile, for the syrup, heat a generous ½ cup water with the sugar and lemon juice in a saucepan. Bring to a boil and simmer for 15 minutes. Chill.

8 Remove the baklava from the oven and allow to cool in the pan. Pour the chilled syrup over the entire pastry. Allow to cool completely before recutting the shapes.

Rice Pudding

SUTLAC

This is one of the country's oldest recipes. It is very nutritious and a good dessert to serve to children. Although I like to serve it with jam, in Turkey it would always be served plain. This version, with a crust on top, is delicious.

Serves 4

1 Tbsp short-grain rice, washed

5 cups milk

1 Tbsp rice flour

1 tsp cornstarch

Generous 1 cup sugar

Ground cinnamon, to decorate (optional)

PREPARATION TIME: **10 MINUTES**
COOKING TIME: **25 MINUTES**

1 Preheat a 375°F oven. Cook the rice in water just to cover. Then heat the milk in a saucepan and add the rice. Bring to a boil and simmer.

2 Mix the rice flour and cornstarch in a bowl with a little water to make a smooth paste, then pour this into the simmering milk, stirring constantly.

3 Add the sugar and stir until the mixture thickens. Divide among four individual ovenproof bowls, and bake in the oven until a light brown crust forms on the top. Sprinkle with cinnamon. Serve hot or cold.

Flour Helva

UN HELVASI

Prepare this traditional dessert beforehand and keep it in the refrigerator ready for a dinner party, but remember to serve it at room temperature.

Serves 6

Generous 1 cup margarine

4 cups flour

½ cup pine nuts

1¼ cups milk

Generous 3 cups sugar

PREPARATION TIME: **30 MINUTES**

1 Melt the margarine and stir in the flour. Keep on stirring over medium heat until the flour is very light brown in color. Add the pine nuts and, still stirring, brown the nuts slightly.

2 Pour over a generous ½ cup water. Boil the milk with the sugar in a separate pan and pour it into the helva mixture. Stir once, cover, and cook over medium heat until all the liquid is absorbed.

3 Stir again and, while still hot, take tablespoon-size pieces out, shape, and serve on individual plates.

◀ *Flour Helva*

Semolina Helva

IRMIK HELVASI

This recipe, like the other helva dishes, dates back to the Ottomans, and is a formal dish usually only cooked on special occasions. It is very light in consistency and delicately flavored by pine nuts.

Serves 6

2¼ sticks butter
2⅔ cups semolina
½ cup pine nuts
5 cups milk or half water,
   half milk
2½ cups sugar
¾ cup confectioners' sugar

PREPARATION TIME: **10 MINUTES**
COOKING TIME: **30 MINUTES**

❶ Melt the butter in a large saucepan, then add the semolina and pine nuts together, and cook until the pine nuts change color, stirring continuously.

❷ Bring the milk to a boil in a separate saucepan and stir in the superfine sugar. Pour the milk over the semolina and pine nuts, stir once, cover, and cook for 3 minutes over high heat, 3 minutes over medium heat, and 3 minutes over low heat, until the milk is absorbed. Allow to stand over very low heat for 10 minutes.

❸ Divide half the helva among six individual dishes and sprinkle with the confectioners' sugar. Then, using a spoon, firm the remaining helva against the side of the pan and arrange it in the individual dishes on top of the other helva. Serve hot or cold.

Fig Dessert

INCIR TATLISI

This is an unusual and delicious dessert from the Aegean, where figs are plentiful. Although simple, it is quite filling.

Serves 4

1 lb dried figs
1 cup chopped mixed nuts
Generous ½ cup sugar
Heavy whipping cream,
or clotted cream, to serve

PREPARATION TIME: **20 MINUTES**
COOKING TIME: **20 MINUTES**

❶ Preheat a 375°F oven and grease an ovenproof dish. Mix together the chopped nuts and sugar.

❷ Cut off the stalks of the figs and, with your fingers, open up the central cavity. Fill each fig with the nut mixture. Place in the ovenproof dish with 1¼ cups hot water. Cook in the oven for 20 minutes, basting occasionally. Allow to cool and serve with the cream.

Fig Dessert ▶

Piped Desserts

TULUMBA TATLISI

If you have a sweet tooth, then this is the recipe for you. It is a very traditional dessert, dating back to the Ottomans. I give the recipe here with less sugar than would normally be used in Turkey.

Serves 4

FOR THE SYRUP
2¼ cups sugar
Juice of ½ lemon

FOR THE PASTRY
1 stick butter
Pinch of salt
1 Tbsp sugar
Generous 2 cups flour
4 eggs
Olive oil, for shallow frying
½ cup shelled pistachios, chopped, to decorate

PREPARATION TIME: **20 MINUTES**
COOKING TIME: **1 HOUR**

1 For the syrup, place the sugar and lemon juice in a large saucepan, add 1¾ cups water, and bring to a boil. Simmer for 15 minutes until thickened slightly. Allow to cool.

2 For the pastry, heat 1¾ cups water in a saucepan and add the butter, a pinch of salt, and the sugar. Bring to a boil and, stirring rapidly, add the flour. Stirring continuously, simmer for 10 minutes, then turn off the heat, and allow to cool. When cool, knead with the eggs.

3 Put a little dough at a time into a large piping bag fitted with a ½ inch star or plain piping nozzle, and pipe lengths of pastry about 2 inches long onto waxed paper.

4 Place the pastries in a skillet with some olive oil. Heat the oil but do not stir. When the pastries harden on one side, turn them over and fry on the second side until golden. Drain, place in a serving dish, pour the cold syrup over the pastries, and sprinkle with the chopped pistachios.

Pumpkin Dessert

KABAK TATLISI

What do you do with the flesh of a Hallowe'en pumpkin? This is a good way to use those shapeless chunks. Scoop out the seeds and then cut the flesh into pieces. Arrange them in a serving dish and sprinkle with the nuts.

Serves 4

2 lb pumpkin
1½ cups sugar
1¼ cups shelled walnuts, chopped
Heavy cream, whipped

PREPARATION TIME: **30 MINUTES**
COOKING TIME: **40 MINUTES**

1 Seed and peel the pumpkin and cut into 5- by 3-inch wide pieces. Arrange in a shallow pan half filled with water. Cook over medium heat until tender.

2 Add the sugar when the liquid is reduced, cover, and cook until the sugar is dissolved. Simmer without the lid until the syrup is thickened.

3 Remove from heat and place in a serving dish. Sprinkle with walnuts and serve cold with cream.

Pumpkin Dessert ▲

Almond Dessert

SEKERPARE

This is a good dessert after a big dinner. When served in individual dishes, it looks neat, pretty, and is delicately sweet.

Serves 4

1 egg

1 egg yolk

Generous $\frac{1}{2}$ cup sugar

2 sticks butter, softened

4 cups flour

A few drops of vanilla extract

About 16 whole blanched almonds

FOR THE SYRUP

Generous 1 cup sugar

Juice of $\frac{1}{2}$ lemon

PREPARATION TIME: **20 MINUTES**
COOKING TIME: **45 MINUTES**

1 For the syrup, put the sugar and lemon juice into a saucepan with a scant 1 cup water, and bring to a boil. Simmer until the syrup thickens, turn off the heat, and allow to cool.

2 Beat the egg and egg yolk with the sugar and add the softened butter. Add the flour and vanilla extract, and mix well.

3 Preheat a 375°F oven and butter an ovenproof dish. Take walnut-size pieces of dough and roll in the palms of your hands to make small balls. Press and flatten slightly. Arrange in the dish, leaving space between. Place an almond in the center of each one. Bake in the oven for 35 minutes, until nicely browned.

4 Pour the syrup over and leave the pastries to cool before placing in a serving dish.

Fruit and Nut Dessert

ASURE

This is one of my favorite desserts. It is rich and nutritious with nuts, figs, raisins, and garbanzo beans. I use pure wheat germ for this recipe which you can obtain from health-food stores. You can instead use any pure wheat cereal. The wheat will incorporate while cooking, but it requires a lot of water. It is a very famous dessert dating back to the Ottomans, when it was cooked in giant casseroles to celebrate the coming of spring.

Serves 6

7 oz natural wheat germ

1 Tbsp kidney or navy beans

1 Tbsp garbanzo beans

1 Tbsp raisins

1 cup sugar

1¹⁄₂ oz shelled, skinned, and
    chopped hazelnuts

3¹⁄₂ oz shelled, skinned, and
    chopped walnuts

4 dried figs, chopped fine

A few drops of rose oil,
    to sprinkle

Seeds of 1 pomegranate,
    to decorate

PREPARATION TIME: **20 MINUTES PLUS
OVERNIGHT SOAKING TIME**
COOKING TIME: **5 HOURS**

Tip

The cooking time for Fruit and Nut Dessert is five hours. To speed things up, you could use a pressure cooker. After soaking the wheat, beans, and raisins overnight, place all the ingredients together in the cooker and cook for 30 minutes.

1 Soak the wheat, beans, garbanzo beans, and raisins overnight.

2 The next day, in a large saucepan, cook the wheat in about 5 pints water. Skim off the foam with a large spoon while boiling. Cover and cook over medium heat for 4 hours, until soft.

3 Cook the navy and garbanzo beans in water separately until soft, according to the package instructions.

4 When the water of the wheat thickens, add the sugar and drained garbanzo and navy beans. Cook for 1 hour more. Remove from the heat and stir in the hazelnuts, walnuts, raisins, and figs.

5 Place in individual dishes and, when cooled, sprinkle with a little rose oil and decorate with pomegranate seeds.

Sweet Rice

ZERDE

The inclusion of saffron makes this such an attractive dish. Its coloring is exquisite and it makes a lovely end to any meal.

Serves 4

Scant ¾ cup short-grain rice

⅔ cup sugar

A few saffron strands

1 Tbsp arrowroot

1 Tbsp currants

1 Tbsp chopped mixed nuts,
   to decorate

Seeds of 1 pomegranate,
   to decorate

PREPARATION TIME: **20 MINUTES**
COOKING TIME: **40 MINUTES**

1 Wash the rice and place in 5 cups water with the sugar. Bring to a boil and simmer for 20 minutes.

2 Soak the saffron in a little warm water, then add to the rice. Dissolve the arrowroot to a smooth paste in a little cold water, then add to the rice with the currants. Mix well and simmer over medium heat for 20 minutes until thickened.

3 Divide the mixture among individual bowls and leave to cool. Sprinkle with chopped nuts and pomegranate seeds, and serve.

Peaches with Raspberry Sauce

SEFTALI TATLISI

This is a wonderful dessert to serve when the fruit are in season. They make a refreshing combination for the end of a meal.

Serves 2

2 fresh peaches, washed

1¼ cups raspberries

¼ cup sugar

Heavy cream, whipped

PREPARATION TIME: **5 MINUTES**
COOKING TIME: **20 MINUTES**

1 In a small saucepan bring 2½ cups water to a boil. Place the washed peaches in the water and lower the heat. Cook gently for 7 minutes, then drain, and peel the peaches. Chill for 2 hours.

2 Place the raspberries in a saucepan with the sugar, mix well, and bring to a boil. Take off the heat and push through a metal sifter to remove the seeds.

3 Place the peaches on a serving dish, with the raspberry sauce spooned over, and a little heavy cream or sour cream.

Chicken Breast Pudding

TAVUK GOGSU

Although sounding strange to newcomers to Turkish cooking, this dessert is simply delicious and I have never known anyone who did not like it. The restaurants on the banks of the Bhosphorus in Istanbul feature it regularly on their menus. The taste is not reminiscent of the chicken at all, but its origins and the idea of using chicken in a milk dessert, are lost in the mists of time.

Serves 4

Half a chicken breast

5 cups milk

Generous 1¼ cups sugar

Salt

1 Tbsp cornstarch

Scant 1 cup rice flour

Ground cinnamon,
   for sprinkling

PREPARATION TIME: **20 MINUTES**
COOKING TIME: **50 MINUTES**

1 Cook the chicken breast in water until tender. Drain and cut crosswise into 2-inch long pieces. Rub these pieces between the palms of your hands and tear into very thin fibers. Soak the fibers briefly in warm water then squeeze them tightly to extract excess water. Repeat twice, changing the water each time.

2 Place the milk, sugar, and some salt in a saucepan and bring to a boil, stirring continuously. Mix the starch and the rice flour with a little of the milk to a smooth paste. Stirring, pour the paste slowly into the milk and simmer until the milk starts to thicken.

3 Add the chicken fibers and reduce the heat. Simmer until thickened, stirring all the time. To check the consistency, pour a little of the mixture onto a plate. Allow to cool and turn the plate upside-down. It should come off completely without sticking to the plate.

4 Pour the mixture into a 1-inch deep serving dish and allow to cool. Cut out four equal portions and roll each one into a cylinder shape. Sprinkle with cinnamon to serve.

Burnt Chicken Breast Pudding

KAZANDIBI

This is a classic of Ottoman cuisine and still very popular. It is served with ice cream in Istanbul and it is truly delicious.

Serves 4

Half a chicken breast

5 cups milk

Generous 1¼ cups sugar

Salt

1 Tbsp cornstarch

Scant 1 cup rice flour

Ground cinnamon,
   for sprinkling

PREPARATION TIME: **50 MINUTES**
PLUS COOLING TIME

1 Prepare the Chicken Breast Pudding (above) but pour the mixture into a heatproof, 1-inch deep dish. Put the dish over a gas flame and brown the underside evenly, moving the pan over the flame if necessary.

2 Allow to cool for 2 hours, then cut it into four equal square pieces. Transfer to a serving dish and fold each piece like a thick roll. Place the browned side upward and sprinkle with cinnamon.

Burnt Chicken Breast Pudding ▶

Fritter Balls

LOKMA

These fried batter balls have syrup poured over before serving. If you prefer, you could dip them in honey.

Serves 4

FOR THE SYRUP

Generous ½ cup sugar

1 Tbsp lemon juice

FOR THE BATTER

1¾ cups flour

2 sachets (½ oz) dried yeast

1 Tbsp butter, melted

Salt

Oil, for shallow frying

Ground cinnamon,
   for sprinkling

PREPARATION TIME: **30 MINUTES**
COOKING TIME: **1 HOUR PLUS STANDING TIME**

Tip

Cook these little dough balls in small batches to ensure the oil retains its heat and the balls quickly acquire a golden brown coating

1 For the syrup, put the sugar and lemon juice in a saucepan with ½ cup water and bring to a boil. Simmer for 15 minutes then take off the heat.

2 Sift the flour into a mixing bowl, then add the yeast, butter, and a little salt. Mix well, then add ¾ cup water gradually while stirring. Make a soft dough and leave in a warm place for 1 hour.

3 Heat the oil in a skillet. Take hazelnut-size pieces of the dough with a wet spoon and fry gently in batches of eight. Remove the balls as they are cooked and drain on paper towels.

4 Fry the balls for a second time until nicely browned, turning occasionally. Drain and pour the syrup over, covering the balls evenly. Then drain again and serve hot sprinkled with cinnamon.

Turkish Delight

LOKUM

I give the better-known rose-water version of these famous candies, dating back to the fifteenth century. You can also make them with the addition of pistachios, almonds, or coconut for a more traditional version.

Makes about 25

2¼ cups sugar

A pinch of cream of tartar or 1 oz gelatin, dissolved in water

Scant ⅓ cup cornstarch

Scant 1 cup confectioners' sugar plus extra for dusting

A few drops of rose water

¼ cup honey

1 Tbsp pistachios, halved

PREPARATION TIME: **20 MINUTES**
COOKING TIME: **1½ HOURS**

1 Put the sugar in a saucepan with ½ cup water. Bring to a boil, stirring until the sugar is dissolved. Boil until the soft ball stage, about 240°F. Drop a little of the syrup into a bowl of cold water; if it forms a ball then it has reached the required temperature.

2 Remove the pan from the heat, stir in the cream of tartar or the dissolved gelatin. Blend the cornstarch and the confectioners' sugar with 3 cups water in another saucepan. Bring to a boil, stirring all the time, then simmer until thickened and clear.

3 Gradually beat the cream of tartar or gelatin mixture into the cornstarch mixture. Bring to a boil, stirring frequently, for at least 30 minutes until transparent.

4 Remove from the heat and stir in the rose water and honey. Pour half of the mixture into a greased 6- by 6-inch, deep, square cake pan. Scatter the nuts over. Pour the remaining half into the pan. Leave in a cool place overnight, or until set.

5 Turn the *lokum* out of the pan and cut into squares with a knife dipped in confectioners' sugar. Dust with more confectioners' sugar to coat the squares well.

Rose Petal Preserve

GUL RECELI

This preserve evokes the delicate scents of a summer's day. It is not brought to setting point, so disregard the usual tests. It tastes delicious with slightly toasted white bread spread with unsalted butter. If you would like a dark color preserve, use dark red fragrant rose petals.

Makes 1 lb

8 oz fragrant pink rose petals

2 pt water

2 lb sugar

Juice of 2 lemons

PREPARATION TIME: **5 MINUTES**
COOKING TIME: **35 MINUTES**

1 Place the rose petals and water in a preserving pan. Cover and bring to a boil. Simmer for 5 minutes then stir in the sugar.

2 Boil rapidly with the lid off for about 20 minutes, until the syrup thickens slightly. Add the lemon juice and bring to a boil once more.

3 Turn off the heat and allow it to cool.

4 Pour into sterilized jars.

Quince Preserve

AYVA RECELI

There is a delicate fragrance to be enjoyed while cooking this preserve, and the beautiful color that graces the breakfast table makes preparing Ayva receli worthwhile.

Makes 1 lb

2 lb yellow quinces

½ pt water

2½ lb sugar

Juice of 1 lemon

PREPARATION TIME: **10 MINUTES**
COOKING TIME: **35 MINUTES**

1 Wash and peel the quinces. Scoop the seeds out and slice thinly.

2 Place in a preserving pan with the water and bring to a boil. Simmer until soft, then stir in the sugar. Simmer until the sugar is dissolved.

3 Add the lemon juice and boil rapidly until set. You can check the set by placing a teaspoon of the preserve on a cold plate. Allow it to cool sufficiently to run a finger through it. If the mixture wrinkles, it is set, if not simmer for a few minutes more and repeat the test.

4 Remove from the heat, allow to cool a little and pour into sterilized jars. Leave to cool completely before sealing the jars.

Yogurt Drink

AYRAN

This is a very simple and refreshing drink, generally served very cold with Doner Kebap, *sandwiches or burgers. It can be purchased ready mixed in bottles or cartons all over Turkey, and locals will flavor the drink by adding fresh fruit of their choice.*

Serves 4

2 cups thick plain yogurt

2 cups cold water

a dash of salt

1 Place all the ingredients in a blender and whisk until frothy.

2 Divide the froth among four glasses, followed by the remainder of the drink.

Sugar Syrup Drink

SHERBET

Traditional sherbets are made from a special sherbet candy which is made from sun drying, molding and pressing mulberries, sour cherries, or flowers such as orchids and roses. This sugar syrup is the base for a variety of sherbets.

Serves 1

SUGAR SYRUP

¼ cup sugar

1 cup water

SHERBET

2 fl oz cherry juice

2 fl oz red grape juice

2 fl oz mulberry juice or exotic fruit juice

2 fl oz grapefruit juice

1 fl oz sugar syrup

Carbonated lemonade or soda water

A few sprigs of mint

A slice of lemon

1 To make the sugar syrup: Dissolve the sugar in water over a moderate heat. Bring to a boil and simmer for 5 minutes. Allow to cool and then pour into a sterilized container. Cover and store in the refrigerator.

2 To make the sherbet: Shake all the ingredients together with a little crushed ice. Pour into a long glass and top up with chilled soda water or lemonade.

Turkish Coffee

Serves 2

To make Turkish coffee correctly does require a long-handled pot called a "cezve." These are made in different sizes, depending on the number of people for whom you are making coffee. If a cezve is not available, try using a small pan which can be placed on the flame, preferably with a long handle to avoid getting burnt while the coffee is boiling. A well-made coffee must have froth on the surface, so do not use too large a pan. You will need to buy either Turkish coffee, which can be found in specialty coffee stores, or have your coffee beans toasted and ground to a fine powder. Serve the coffee in tiny cups, with Turkish Delight.

1 tsp superfine sugar, optional
2 tsp Turkish coffee

1 Measure cold water, by using the coffee cups, into the cezve. Stir in the sugar and bring slowly to a boil over a low heat.

2 Add the coffee, stir well and heat until the froth forms on top. Just at the moment it may overflow, remove from the heat and divide the froth into the cups.

3 Return the cezve to the heat and bring to a boil again.

4 Pour the remaining coffee into the cups and serve hot.

INDEX